D1561038

Sharing the Old, Old Story

Sharing the Old, Old Story:
Educational Ministry in the Black Community

Nathan Jones

Saint Mary's Press
Christian Brothers Publications
Winona, Minnesota

Size2
BX
930
.J66
1982
2 8.43
J722

82 111542

Dr. Nathan Jones has had years of experience in adult education in Catholic parishes, and his background includes many well-received workshops and talks to various Christian groups. He was formerly a staff member of the Archdiocese of Chicago and is presently a consulting editor for Ethnic Communications Outlet in Chicago and a lecturer in Black religious studies at Mundelein College. **Sharing the Old, Old Story** is designed, as Dr. Jones says, "to affirm and strengthen Black people in their spirituality and, at the same time, to help retool White people for working with Blacks."

The original concept of this book was born at Ethnic Communications Outlet, Chicago. E.C.O. is a communications ministry of the Society of the Divine Word (S.V.D.) E.C.O. creates print and mass media programs in response to the religious and community needs of minority communities.

Ethnic Communications Outlet
5342 South University Avenue
Chicago, IL 60615 (312) 667-2626

Illustrations by Robert Trammell (cover and pages 14, 30, 56, 70, 82, 92, 104) and Therese A. Gasper (pages 16, 20, 21, 22, 23, 84, 85); photographs by James Leibner, S.V.D.

ISBN: 0-88489-144-5
Library of Congress Catalog Card Number: 81-86046
Copyright 1982 by Saint Mary's Press,
Terrace Heights, Winona, Minnesota 55987.

Contents

One of the greatest gifts of the Church is age. As the centuries have unfolded, we the Church have learned much about what it means to be saved. So we can tell this old, old Story. Yet each generation and culture retells the Story with a distinction and a freshness because each has experienced the Story somewhat differently.

This book has been shaped by many people of several generations—folk just like you who have openheartedly shared with me their stories, insights, questions—all kinds of creativity—concerning the awesome mission of breaking open the life-giving Good News of Jesus Christ.

Recognition is one of the great marks of creativity. When I recognize something of my own life-pilgrimage and daily efforts in a particular work of art, the artist has successfully spoken.

For instance, a popular group of singing Black women have said, "I've been down so long, up ain't even crossed my mind. . . ." How accurately descriptive this revelation of the people's condition is. I am made forcibly conscious that the God of the Bible who hears the cry of the oppressed surely hears and sees the wreckage of human life and the countless destructive forces which prevail against those who are Black, vulnerable, and poor.

A close examination of the people's condition, as well as an ongoing strengthening of ministerial skills, are at the heart of this book. Truly we must not only tell the folk about the old, old Story of the Church but, equally as important, we must share with them an *experience* of Church they can actually *feel,* an enduring experience they will never forget.

The Old, Old Story

Story—storytelling and listening—is a central methodology of catechetical ministry. Story is not simply a passing, present-day interest of the religious community, but rather an attempt to recover a lost emphasis. Christian faith did not originally come to us as theology. The Good News came to us as story: "In the beginning . . ."

As the ages have unfolded, this Story has become a cherished tradition handed on down the generations with care. In the Hebrew Scriptures we read the *shema* ("Hear, O Israel"), recorded in Deut. 6:4-9, a passage celebrating the source of life within the nation Israel.

> Hear, O Israel! The Lord is our God, the Lord alone! Therefore, you shall love the Lord, your God, with all your heart, and with all your soul, and with all your strength. Take to heart these words which I enjoin on you today. Drill them into your children. Speak of them at home and abroad, whether you are busy or at rest. Bind them

foundations and practical insights here. If you are a minister of religious education (DRE/DCE), catechist, minister or pastor, divinity student, Black or non-Black, Catholic-Christian or Protestant-Christian, or simply a person seeking faith-enrichment, information, and perhaps inspiration, this guide has been developed with you in mind.

Following are some of the main functions this guide was designed to fulfill:

• While exegeting our times, while listening to our ancestral spirits, and while recalling the journey of Black people, we will continually ask: *"What is the word that is ours to speak on behalf of Black people?"* By uncovering this "word" we will be enabled to reverence, express, and effectively **communicate faith in a language understandable by Black people.** Efforts to adapt religious education materials designed for other communities to Black people have largely proved to be dysfunctional. Instead, by dipping into the treasure of the Afrikan and Afrikan-American encounter with God, we can discover a new context, a message, and a medium which speaks to Black life.

• To help provide the individual catechist with the tooling and retooling necessary to appreciate the distinctive dimensions of sharing faith in the Black church, this book can **serve as a source for personal reflection and ministerial evaluation.**

• Efforts to form catechists in Black parishes frequently have failed because standard teacher training materials were inadequate. *Sharing the Old, Old Story,* unlike other such guides, is grounded in the conviction that catechists should be exposed to the very soul of Black religious experience as the starting point for their ministry. For catechist formation programs on the diocesan or local levels, which bring together persons involved in similar educational ministries, this book can **serve as a primary resource of Black religious experience.**

• For any supportive learning group, the material in this book will function on two levels: (1) to **initiate a process of dialogue** and formation between the master catechist and those in training and (2) to **offer a systematic introduction** to the distinctive tasks of catechetical ministry in the Black community.

The benefits of these two purposes are diverse, reflecting the best of contemporary educational theory, especially as espoused by Brazilian educator, Paulo Freire. The dialogical methodology functions to enable all persons involved to share from the wealth of their life-experiences. Human life and experience form the common starting point. From a catechetical perspective, this process is well substantiated in Thomas Groome's germinative work, *Christian Religious Education: Sharing Our Story and Vision.*

• Furthermore, this book has been designed around core concepts which **form an organic approach to growth in faith as well as education for liberation.** Therefore, catechists-in-formation will be exposed to the broad spectrum of concerns of which they must be informed while being sensitized to the dimensions most related to Black faith-growth.

Catechist Formation Sessions

Because catechists are often volunteers from the local church, it is imperative that parishes and dioceses provide ongoing training opportunities at regular intervals to enrich and enliven the teaching itself. These formation sessions can meet at church facilities or even within homes or community institutions for the convenience of the participants.

The master catechist should insist on a conducive environment for adult learning, including a well-lighted space with comfortable furnishings. Such materials as audio-visuals, easels, writing equipment, or charts should be readily available.

Catechist formation sessions as outlined in this guide include the following components:

1) An informal section designed to introduce each chapter and to initiate reflection upon individual, ministerial successes and struggles (utilizing especially the sections on "Personal Responses").

2) An opportunity to focus on the topic at hand, using the INITIATION activities to precipitate personal reflection. (As you study this manual initially, you should do these activities yourself.)

3) A prepared and structured presentation by the master catechist of the chapter's essential content offered at a level the participants can easily find helpful and not overwhelming. This will require that the leader comprehend and absorb the material in the PRESENTATION sections.
Note well: The master catechist will take on much of the teaching responsibilities during the first three sessions as they are outlined here. This is due to the fact that the first formation sessions require substantial input from an experienced teacher of the Word. In the later sessions, however, the thrust of the material shifts more and more to the roles and responsibilities of the learners themselves.

4) Group and individual activities aimed at a fuller grasp of the content and its implications (see sections on INTEGRATION). These activities can be presented to the group by the master catechist.

5) A concluding experience of worship, ritual, and sharing of refreshments as a form of celebration in order to support the network of fellowship (see CELEBRATION sections).

6) A summary of the main points of the chapter (see RESPONSE sections) followed by an opportunity to reconsider your "Personal Responses" in light of the new insights presented in each chapter.

Like movements in music, each chapter constitutes a gradual unfolding of the larger picture. Good Black music also requires improvisation, that is, the capacity to more and more deeply penetrate the focal theme. Likewise, consider these chapters merely a seed which will necessarily require watering, tending, as well as pastoral and cultural adaptations based on your local needs.

My firm hope is that by enhancing our ministries we will begin to undo the ravages of racism, self-hate, and despair. And by claiming the stories of our Blood and Faith we will become empowered to denounce whatever denies life while announcing the marvelous inbreaking into *our* Story of the God who binds broken hearts and sets the oppressed free.

I wish to profoundly thank all the many, many persons—family and friends—who have loved and nurtured me while challenging me to ask the right questions. Only the mistakes have been mine. A special thanks to Reverend Derek Simons, SVD, and Stephan Nagel, whose editorial assistance and patience were major forces in bringing this project to completion.

That which is good is never finished.

—Sukuma proverb

Nathan W. Jones

1
The Roots of Black Catechesis

The essential and distinct qualities of catechesis in the Black community are that Black people are a pilgrim people, a biblical people, a faith community, and a people of vision. Everything we do is shaped and informed by these qualities.

Jesus, spiritually invigorated . . . went to church on Sunday. They invited him to preach, so he got up to read the scripture and found the place in the book of Isaiah where it says:

"The Lord's spirit is on me:
he has ordained me to break the good news
to the poor people.
He has sent me to proclaim freedom
for the oppressed,
and sight for the blind,
to help those who have been grievously insulted
to find dignity;
to proclaim the Lord's new era."

Clarence Jordan
The Cotton Patch Version of Luke

How is it possible to deal with the center of the Black experience and history . . . without coming to terms with the most visible faith of the people?

James H. Cone

This learning experience aims to enable you:

TO KNOW   To identify the distinctive elements of catechesis in the Black community.

TO FEEL	To grasp a heightened sense of what it is to be Black Catholic-Christian in community with others.
TO DO	To begin to articulate a personal vision of the Black church's educational ministry.

Now, before reading further, turn to the section, "Personal Responses," on page 26.

INITIATION: Your Kind of Church

An Exercise

Find a comfortable spot and, with a blank sheet of paper and several marker pens at hand, prepare for this introspective exercise. Draw a series of clouds on the sheet of paper leaving enough space inside each cloud to later write a word.

Ask yourself: "What *atmosphere* would I like to see in my church (school, church-related institution, or community)?" As word-images surface for you, take a different colored marker pen and write the word in the center of one of the clouds until each cloud is named. If you are doing this exercise with others, spend time exchanging the reasons behind each choice of word-images.

After each cloud has been identified, draw a large, brightly colored, rising sunburst at the bottom of the paper.

This rising sun symbol is a constant reminder that if we seek an atmosphere of peace, love, understanding, cooperation, devotion, honesty, etc., within our church or community, it begins with *us*.

> For it is not your *aptitude*
> that determines your *altitude,*
> but your *attitude,*
> with a teaspoon of intestinal fortitude.

Spend some time in silent reflection carefully studying your project and searching for the application of this message to you and your educational ministry. If you have participated in this project with others, take a few minutes to discuss the significance of these insights for your shared ministry.

A Reflection

In order to guide Black people toward a deeper appreciation of the Christian faith that "propped up their ancestors on every leaning side," we must first take a hard look at the basics. Basics refer to the roots, the grounding, the foundation out of which grows all else we say and do.

A perceptive reading of the times gives us the assurance that we can no longer afford to neglect the distinctive needs of Black people for an informed faith, a growing faith. The continuing realities of economic depression, escalating unemployment, political mismanagement, religious profiteerism, and the new-style racism called "reverse discrimination" stand out as glaring evidence that the people must be aimed by and armed with a faith that does justice.

Therefore, without any romanticism, we plunge headlong into the task of discovering the foundational principles which will give substance, direction, and credibility to our catechetical ministries in the Black community.

PRESENTATION A: The Five-Point Black Position Statements

All the beliefs, traditions, actions, celebrations, efforts, and plans of the Black Christian community must be aimed toward a fuller, more abundant life for the entire people. This is the meaning of the Church as a liberating and saving community.

In the book *The Challenge of Blackness* by Lerone Bennett, the profound challenge is issued that we must "believe in the community of the Black dead and the Black living and the Black unborn. We [must] believe that that community has a prior claim on our time and our talents and our resources, and that we must respond when it calls."

To be liberation-oriented in our educational ministry means that our thrust is toward the freedom and new life that is God's indescribable gift (2 Cor. 9:15). For the Church's catechetical ministry to be liberation-oriented it must embody these five key principles. Although this chapter and subsequent chapters will raise up other principles and affirmations, the "Five-Point Black Position Statements" are clearly basic. Out of the substance of these statements all other principles flow.

The Five-Point Black Position Statements

1) To build an identity in a people (a sense of *who* you are and *whose* you are).
2) To enable a people to discern God's movement in their personal and collective stories and to celebrate their pilgrimage.
3) To develop a perspective toward love, justice, truth, reconciliation, and freedom.
4) To take a position: clearly choose sides where the life and future of a people are concerned, based on the Gospel values stated above.
5) To share the community's living faith in Christ Jesus, its traditions, and its ritual celebrations—ever mindful of the connections to the real-life conditions of the people.

These five position statements function to: (a) provide a **basic, predictable pattern and structure** to the total educational ministry of the Black church; (b) provide a **language** through which we can more appropriately articulate the clarifications, specifications, and expectations which are uniquely Black; (c) provide **scaffolding** to support creative endeavors generated on the local level; and (d) set a **horizon** for the Black church's widely conceived teaching ministry.

These position statements are guidelines for educational ministry in the Black community. By offering our efforts a framework, these statements will assist us in giving shape and contour to catechesis from a Black perspective.

These five steps seek to enable the present-day Black church to employ the same historic principles in its catechetical ministry that gave birth and momentum to the origins of the Black church in America.

INTEGRATION A: Owning the Principles

An Exercise

Your task is now to rewrite each of the five Black position statements (on p. 18) using the language, idiom, symbols, and insights of your local community. In other words, how can we so rephrase these five positions or principles that they can truly be our own, truly *live for us?*

If you have been engaged in this activity with others, you might proceed as follows:

The participants will form discussion groups and, after a few moments of individual reflection, will share their ideas with each other. A recorder comes forth from each group and shares the statements one by one. Someone should record these on newsprint so they are visible to all.

After each group has shared, the task remains to arrive at a consensus among *all* participants regarding each statement. The assembly will make a circle (fishbowl) around the recorders, who are charged to discuss the statements until a consensus in language, style, and concept is reached. Remarks can be made by members of the larger body in order to move the consensus process with questions, clarifications, and specifications. When a consensus is reached, these statements are proudly proclaimed by the recorders.

The statement paper is placed on a small table near the enthroned Bible and, if possible, each catechist approaches and signs his/her name on the sheet. Through this ritual action, all persons affirm these principles as goals and agree to be informed by them in their ministries.

PRESENTATION B: Foundations

Flowing from the "Five-Point Black Position Statements," there are several necessary elements and ingredients in the shaping of catechesis in the Black Catholic church community. Each component is inseparably linked to the others and each component necessarily implies the others. Furthermore, these elements are not an exhaustive listing. Your own local church experience might indicate to you new thrusts as yet undreamed in the following ingredients. In this way you are actively participating in the ongoing creation of life-giving and effective teaching/learning models which truly respond to the felt needs of your community.

I strongly believe that no catechetical program in the Black community can hope to flourish if any of these components are missing or weakly implemented. Therefore, these components function as guiding principles for all such formational-educational pursuits in the Black church.

1) Black Pilgrimage

A while ago I visited a Black church that was well known for its lively worship and thriving congregational life. I had suspected I would find there a creative blending of the Gospel with the heritage and culture of the people. I left disappointed.

This church had done what many other Black faith communities, across denominational lines, have consistently done. They separated the biblical story from the Black story. Every Sunday when this church gathered, they drew upon cultural symbols, behavior, and ritual expressions that were unmistakably Afrikan in origin. For the most part, the chants, colorful uniforms, protocol, religious language, and spirit possession grew out of Afrika. Yet while the biblical story was told with a drama and emotion distinctly Afrikan, an explicit retelling of the Black story (heritage, culture, contemporary issues, values) was absent. The two stories appeared to be unrelated, and nobody was asking questions concerning the appropriateness of the situation.

If Black churches are once again to reclaim their historic freedom-orientation, significant strides to reconnect the biblical-Black stories must be made. Indeed, they are not two stories but rather one continual flowering of God's revelation.

Catechesis must build, then, on life and on the day-to-day experiences of real people. Our catechesis must endeavor to uncover the Good News in daily living: Where are God's messages in the raw details and dailiness of our lives? This is precisely our starting point.

"Black pilgrimage" is about empowering persons to get in touch with their own personal stories—the highlands and lowlands—and to claim them. Without a doubt, such formation develops a sense of worth, self-esteem, and self-respect in adults, youth, and children.

The poet and institution-builder Haki R. Madhubuti, in his outstanding book *From Plan to Planet,* establishes these three criteria for Blackness: **color, culture,** and **consciousness.** Based on these criteria, catechesis necessarily involves concrete efforts to cleanse the minds of the hearers from a slave mentality of self-hatred to a love of self and others like one's self. Unless we can initiate the long walk toward accepting our truest selves, we will not be fully open to receive God's freeing Word.

What is the word spoken on the backporches, front stoops, or in the alleys? What messages accompany the rhythms from the radios and stereos? What happens at the laundromats, kitchen tables, or at the corner grocery stores? What troubles have visited the people and taken a seat and stayed awhile? In short, what are the folk talking and singing about, and what feelings and concerns are "on the people's hearts"?

We as churchgoers do a lot of talking, but this foundational principle requires that we begin to listen. By identifying the strengths and values which emerge out of the Black experience, that give a people renewed energy and purpose for living, we are building up a sense of community among God's people. It is by standing back from daily experience and reflecting upon it that each of us is more fittingly equipped to act.

Reflection on the Black pilgrimage leads us to *make connections* between the lived Christian faith, Scripture, the Church's tradition and worship, and the life-story of Black people. For example, the Black cultural adaptation of the extended family (where if one eats, all eat; if one has a home, all have a home) is invariably related to the New Testament concept of *koinonia,* fellowship where we enter as strangers and leave as friends.

To be a Black and pilgrim people means:
to be connected to all God's sojourners who have journeyed before us, especially our ancestors in the Blood. They have passed on the flame of faith and freedom. We are one with them.

To be a Black and pilgrim people means:
the life and breath of the people are dependent on the One who has made them. As God's *anawim,* we stand under the Word ever disposed to listen and receive from the generous hand of God.

To be a Black and pilgrim people means:
to be always on the way, unfinished, never perfect until we, out of our exile, come home. Be patient; God's not finished with us yet!

2) Vision

Someone raises the question: "So what does Christian faith say to folks who have to deal with the mean, untempered streets; absentee landlords; crowded public transportation; insensitive employers; miseducation in the classrooms; and often ill-prepared parents?" Does our confession of Christ Jesus speak a word of comfort?

If our educational ministry has any ultimate meaning, it will concretely say something to the daily burdens, pleasures, cries, and struggles of hurting people. Admittedly, the poor are those who do not have the freedom to be otherwise, but does Christian faith offer any answers, a direction, a "where" to go?

Catechists and pastoral ministers must guide their communities toward "a reason for the hope that is within you" (Rom. 13:11). If we have found a better way in Christ, the world needs to know this much too well-kept secret.

While some religious educators cart coffee and candles from suburb to suburb, filling up balloons and denying the need for real conversion in people's lives, we must be convinced that all romanticism stops here. It is imperative that we offer some Gospel alternatives to depression, street violence, marriage difficulties, the absence of vital male images, and other

crippling problems of life. Our message begins and ends where the people *are.*

Brazilian educator, Paulo Freire, points out in his powerful book, *Pedagogy of the Oppressed,* that "in order for the oppressed to be able to wage the struggle for their liberation they must perceive the reality of oppression not as a closed world from which there is no exit, but as a limiting situation which they can transform."

To be a people of vision is to believe:
that without a dream or hope to cling to, a people perish.

To be a people of vision is to believe:
that despite evil in high places and our death-dealing world, we hold fast to the Gospel vision of dying and rising.

To be a people of vision is to believe:
that despite the all-embracing evils, God's loving promise of a Kingdom of peace will be realized. It will be there that all peoples will sit at the welcome table, filled, healed, and made whole.

3) Bible

Catechesis in the Black community must be rooted in the Bible, or Black folk will not accept it as "Christian education." It has been said, "If you're goin' to preach to us, make it very plain, daddy, where God said it first. If you ain't talkin' from him, you ain't talkin' nuthin'."

Most Black adults grew up in families where the family Bible was displayed in a place of honor and was truly a "book of the family." Unlike too many households today where the Bible sits among the other dusty books on a shelf, these adults grew up in homes where the Bible was read, reverenced, and frequently quoted.

The kergymatic movement in catechetics and the advances in scriptural studies have enabled Catholics once again to dip into the rich treasures of God's Word. Establishing this principle is helpful, especially in the light of the die-hard story that the Catholic Church discouraged private Bible reading. Officially this was never true; local pastoral practice may have been yet another matter.

Many Blacks, some of whom were first introduced to the old, old Story in Bible-believing, Protestant churches, carry with them memorized biblical passages, stories, images, and prayers and call upon these in times of special need. By identifying and celebrating God's activity in our daily lives, we make God truly present among us.

To be a biblical people means:
to allow the living Word to nourish and inspire us, in season and out of season.

To be a biblical people means:
to understand the Scripture through study and in its meanings for today. To avoid the simplistic, fundamentalist approach to the Bible, we must search out opportunities to grow in our biblical understanding.

To be a biblical people means:
to accept the gripping, double-edged challenge of the Word. This very Word was appropriated by our ancestors and its relevance articulated for our freedom struggle. We also are at peace in the comforting assurance that our people's perception of life and history begins and ends with God.

4) Community of Faith

There are few human experiences that can so powerfully electrify my soul as to share fully in the jubilant joy of Black worship. These moments of pure ecstacy explode in the midst of a spiritual community of oppressed people.

In order for Christian faith to live it must be nurtured within a community. You have been asked, as I have: "Why do you participate in the life of the Church? For, aren't churches boldly hypocritical?" The answer should be unequivocally, "Yes."

Yes, churches have "bought into" the basic myths and assumptions of a racist and sick society. The Church—like the other institutions of business, education, family, and politics—is quite guilty. However, the Church stands forth as a community of sinners saved by grace, and this makes the difference.

Within the Church, meaningful and supportive relationships exist and are fostered. Even small tokens, when given in a supportive environment, can express this caring, mutual affirmation. Children are rewarded with attendance banners in church school, while the youth are honored through scholarship banquets. Adults who have ministered to one another as lectors, soloists, elders, outreach ministers, ushers, church nurses, and committee chairpersons receive corsages or boutonnieres. Everyone is affirmed. The struggles, charisms, spiritual quests, and mutual concerns of all ages are shared.

For Black persons who embrace the Roman Catholic way and tradition of being Christian, liturgy becomes the focus of the community's life. Faith as lively worship is the highest moment in our congregational life. **Liturgy presupposes and needs community, just as it reflects and expresses the community's story, memory, beliefs, values, and lifestyles.**

Outside the Church we would not know the stories of countless unsung believers struggling to make God real in their lives: elderly people, single parents, the sick, and the poor. The church community enables us to bump up against others which is a good way to be reminded that God's blessings extend beyond our own limited grasp into the lives of others.

The Black church is that unique community of believers in Jesus Christ, beyond traditional and denominational lines, brought together by
>   a common blood,
>   a common bondage, and
>   a common new birth.

Although all Black theologians or researchers of Black religion would not fully agree with this definition, I have found this definition helpful in validating as authentic the religious experiences of Blacks in such diverse church settings as Roman Catholic, AME, Church of God in Christ, and storefront assemblies.

By reclaiming this rich legacy, today's Black churches can again be revival and deliverance centers for a weary people. Once again, persons can leave our Sunday liturgies exclaiming, "I feel clean all over!"

To be Church means:
we affirm that there is no such thing as a "private" faith. We journey to God together.

To be Church means:
we affirm that the cornerstone of Christian faith is to be for others. God does have a human face.

To be Church means:
we affirm that the Christian community gifts us with a common language, stories, and symbols with which to articulate and live our faith.

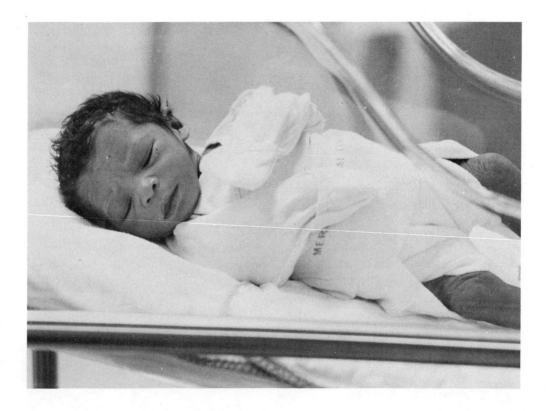

INTEGRATION B: The Hard Questions

Consider the qualities of Black pilgrimage, vision, Bible, and community of faith relative to your own teaching and your parish catechetical ministry.

Spend some time reflecting on and noting the most outstanding strengths and weaknesses of your catechetical ministries. Some possible strengths might be: a sense of congregational ownership, high and consistent attendance, or enriched community life.

On the other hand, some possible weaknesses could be a lack of any of the above or a failure to adequately plan, incompetent leadership, poor advertisement, limited equipment, mediocre methodology, or a low level of expectancy.

Consider these positive and negative qualities in the light of your parish mission statement or the diocesan catechetical standards and policies. Ask yourself: *Are persons knowing, feeling, and doing what we originally envisioned? Why? Why not?*

CELEBRATION: A Bible Enthronement Ceremony

In a dimly lighted room the catechists gather, standing in a semicircle, holding unlit candles. All join in singing a commonly known song, lifting up the theme of light: e.g., "Walk in the Light, Beautiful Light."

While the community sings, a large Bible is reverently carried in procession and accompanied by a candle. As the Bible is opened at the scriptural shrine, the community continues to sing. The individual candles are lit from the processional candle as the hymn is quietly hummed.

A reader comes forth and proclaims the Scripture, saying, "Fellow ministers, a reading from Paul's letter to the church at Ephesus" (6:10-20). At the conclusion of the reading, the community responds, "Thanks be to God!" Following a moment of silent stillness with candles burning, all join again in singing the hymn of light.

RESPONSE: Growing with the Principles

In this chapter we have taken a close look at the catechetical event in the Black faith community with its most basic elements being:

Black pilgrimage (identity),
the Word and tradition (Bible),
community of faith (Church),
vision (direction for life).

Although these elements are not exhaustive of the possible pivotal ingredients for the effective communication of faith in *your* local community, the above-mentioned elements are at least a beginning. Through years of participation in the struggle of building the Black church and through dialogue with the people and the Church's tradition, new elements might emerge to enrich these seeds.

Hopefully, you have completed this chapter with a renewed commitment to calling the Black church to life, especially through your own teaching ministry. By articulating your personal and collective understandings, it is further hoped that these perspectives will truly be *your own.*

Personal Responses

Directions: Before and after reading each chapter, complete the statements or respond to the remarks in the "Personal Responses" section for that chapter. Jotting down your gut-level feelings and attitudes *before* your study of the chapter will enable you to surface your personal agenda and concerns relative to the chapter topics. Returning to these identical sentences *after* your reading may cause you to see your original ideas challenged or affirmed. This activity is aimed at assisting you in clarifying your ideas, attitudes, and feelings as you strive toward greater ministerial effectiveness.

1) "Blackness" to me means . . .

2) "Christian" to me means . . .

3) "Education" to me means . . .

4) Why do we have to open up old wounds by recalling the Afrikan slave trade, racism, social injustice, and other such emotional issues? Theology is objective, like religious education, and does not recognize color or one's political position in the world. I agree . . . I disagree . . .

5) As a Black religious educator, my main task is . . .

6) As a White religious educator ministering in a Black community, my main task is . . .

TEACHING / LEARNING RESOURCES

BOOKS

Freire, Paulo. *Pedagogy of the Oppressed.* New York: Seabury Press, 1970.

Groome, Thomas H. *Christian Religious Education: Sharing Our Story and Vision.* San Francisco: Harper & Row, 1980.

Madhubuti, Haki R. *From Plan to Planet.* Chicago: Third World Press, 1973.

Marthaler, Berard, OFM Conv. *Catechetics in Context.* Huntington, IN: Our Sunday Visitor, 1973.

Sharing the Light of Faith: National Catechetical Directory for Catholics of the United States. Washington, DC: United States Catholic Conference, 1979.

United States Catholic Bishops. *Brothers and Sisters to Us* (U.S. Bishops' Letter on Racism). Washington, DC: United States Catholic Conference, 1979.

ARTICLES

Jones, Nathan. "The Liberation-Oriented Educational Ministry of the Church." *City of God: A Journal of Urban Ministry,* Winter 1979.

_____ . "Problems of Black Catholics." *Religion Teacher's Journal,* October 1977.

Marthaler, Berard, OFM Conv. "Socialization as a Model for Catechetics." In *Foundations of Religious Education,* edited by Padraic O'Hare. New York: Paulist Press, 1978.

Russell, Letty. "Doing Liberation Theology with All Ages." *Church Educator,* February 1978.

Thomas, George B. "Religious Education and Liberation: The Black Minority Mission." *Military Chaplains' Review,* Fall 1978.

MEDIA

"New Roads to Faith: Black Perspectives in Church Education." Produced by Yvonne V. Delk. Filmstrip with record or cassette. The United Church of Christ Press, Joint Educational Development, 1505 Race Street, Philadelphia, PA 19102.

2
Seizing the Beautiful: Black Aesthetics and the Learning Process

Aesthetics in catechesis creates the context in which spiritual values are evoked in the participant responsive to the creations of Black people.

Look at the birds flying around:
they do not plant seeds, gather a harvest,
and put it in barns;
your Father in heaven takes care of them!
Aren't you worth much more than birds?
Look how the wild flowers grow . . .

Matthew 6:26-28

Open your ears to spirit sounds
Open your ears to secret words
Open your mind to spirit songs
Open your soul to receive
Spirits of your family
Spirits of your kind
Spirits of yourself
Sounds of the secret places
Songs of the invisible spaces
Come, sing the warm songs sung
in the inner self . . .

Ed Bullins
from "Spirit Enchantment"

When handed a lemon
make lemonade.
There's always a use for lemon juice . . .

Gwendolyn Brooks

This learning experience aims to enable you:

TO KNOW — To discover some of the aesthetic dimensions of Black life highlighted in the congregational life, message, worship, and ministry of the Black church.

TO FEEL — To realize that even in oppressed communities the Beautiful is clearly manifest and can be creatively employed in the Church's teaching/learning.

TO DO — To demonstrate creative ways in which to integrate the Church's message with the indigenous beauty and culture of the people.

Turn to the "Personal Responses" on page 54.

INITIATION

Important questions to critically examine when searching for a Christian education curriculum or materials for Black communities of faith:

1) Does the curriculum foster an authentic image of the Black male, female, family, and church?
2) Does the curriculum aid people in their search for their cultural roots?
3) Does it show an understanding of the growth and development of the Black child, youth, and adult?
4) Does the curriculum meet the needs of the people in content and skills? Does it reflect and acknowledge the people's experiences?
5) Does the curriculum strengthen your teaching skills as a catechist?
6) Are cultural, ethnic, racial, and religious groups described in a manner to foster understanding, acceptance, empathy, and respect?
7) Does the curriculum seek to motivate learners to examine their own attitudes and behavior, to comprehend their own duties and responsibilities, and to demand freedom, justice, and liberation from oppressive forces and structures in society?

8) Does the curriculum confront the learner with his/her racial, ethnic, and cultural identity and what it means to be a Black Christian in America?
9) Does the curriculum foster within the learner a positive self-concept?

Step one:
Closely examine the nine questions listed above in the light of your parish catechetical goals and objectives.

Step two:
Study the questions listed above, keeping in mind your religious education textbooks and materials (teacher guides, media, and resources) and the need to develop criteria for their selection and use.

PRESENTATION A: Black Aesthetics and Catechesis

The Nguzo Saba (Seven Principles of Black Unity)* lifts up the principle of **KUUMBA/CREATIVITY** and defines it in this manner:

> To do as much as we can,
> in the way we can,
> to leave our community more beautiful
> and beneficial than we inherited it.

In communities of unrest, raging unemployment, inadequate housing, poverty, and unending life-crisis, the discovery of the Beautiful might be essentially impossible for someone without what the genius-musician Stevie Wonder refers to as "inner vision."

Where among the brokenness, pain, hardship, shattered dreams, and gripping oppression could one expect to find any expression of harmony, loveliness, mystery, or the revelation of a creating-liberating-sustaining God?

Countee Cullen, a shining Black poet, captures the irony of this question when he raises his voice: "Yet do I marvel at this curious thing: To make a poet Black, and bid him sing!"

For a person with the eyes to see and the ears to hear, the evidence of the Beautiful and the aesthetic is clearly present even amid seeming contradictions, ugliness, distortions, and disorder.

---

*For an adapted listing of the Nguzo Saba see page 110-111.

Black Aesthetics Defined

Aesthetics is the name we give to the beautiful qualities buried everywhere and to our sensitive response to them. Aesthetics involves a romance with the "Beautiful" and acknowledges the sacramentality of the world.

Black literary critic Stephen Henderson has pointed out in his noteworthy book, *Understanding the New Black Poetry,* "the 'beautiful' is bound up with the truth of a people's history, *as they perceive it themselves,* and if their vision is clear, its recording just, others may perceive that justness too; and, if they bring to it the proper sympathy and humility, they may even share in the general energy, if not the specific content of that vision."

To put this into theological language, our corporate worship is an expression of the life of our community. The Eucharist, for instance, is an expression of the community's living faith—a community that has already been formed. Eucharist does not create community; Eucharist flows out of and back into the community. Similarly, the Black aesthetic is a reflection of the Black story. The Black aesthetic flows out of and back into the Black experience.

Christian educational ministry in the Black community must advocate as an operational principle that *everything* in the people's lives must be seized upon to reinforce, challenge, affirm, and nurture the lives of the people. All of Black life is, therefore, revelatory of the inner wealth of an oppressed and stolen people, while it also speaks intensely of God's abiding presence through it all.

The catechist and minister of the Word possess the awesome task of discerning, in dialogue with the folk, exactly what is God's Word for *this* moment, with *this* community, in *this* particular social reality.

The Black aesthetic has been forged in the fire and by the flame. It has been in the process of living that Black folk have dared to be creative and boldly expressive of their inner beauty and visions in ways which border on the biblical in clarity, insight, and depth, with a particular Black accent, while speaking to the heart of the world.

Many sterling Black voices—imagemakers—have striven to offer positive direction as Black people seek to define themselves, their realities, and their images as distinct from the stereotypes, false images, and distortions which an oppressive society imposes upon them.

The basic social reality of Black people in America is that of an oppressed and colonized people. Ostensibly, this implies that false images are given to Blacks by others—White media, Hollywood, and "negro" disc jockeys on the airwaves.

Ordinary things and actions can be blessed—leading us beyond ourselves and our present situation to higher visions. Making cornbread, washing dishes, gardening, housecleaning, lovemaking, driving a car, painting, or jogging can evoke in us a life-giving response, a sense of wholeness, an encounter with truth if we are but attentive to their messages. **Each moment is pregnant with the Beautiful if we allow it to be born.**

Black Religious Experience and Its Implications for Catechesis

What follows is a schema of the religious expectations of Black people using descriptive phrases and connected to implications for our teaching ministry. This schema, hopefully, will provide a clearer understanding of a few difficult-to-grasp pedagogical insights when ministering with Black people.

Black religious experience characterized by the following descriptive phrases . . .	Implications for catechesis in Black communities . . .
1) "I have come to *feel* God's presence near." Emphasis on the **subjective and intuitive** (feeling) rather than on the objective, abstract, rational thinking.	1) Emphasizes warm, intimate learning experiences. Christian education is an occasion for true learning as well as community. Catechesis should lead persons to experience a new name.
2) "Make it plain, baby!" **Inductive** rather than deductive; emphasis on the concrete.	2) Serious concern for lively presentations, storytelling, drama, and arts in catechesis with a special attention given to the relationship of message to life.
3) "Reach out and touch your neighbor . . ." **Relational:** concerned about daily life-experiences and how they relate to theology and vice versa. Theology as well as catechesis uninformed by daily life is virtually meaningless.	3) Emphasis on participatory learning where everybody has a role. Relationships in the learning community are taken seriously, enriching the quality of the session. We are all lifelong learners in the school of faith. Testifying gives persons confidence in community, removes barriers between self, God, and others, while it edifies the hearers.
4) "Let go and let God." **Circular** rather than linear in our approach to communication.	4) Openness to spontaneity and God's movement, especially in celebration and prayer. Less emphasis on printed materials and greater emphasis on creating a prayerful mood, calling forth the learner's deepest

needs and bringing these to prayer. No one is hurried. The order of the worship service or liturgy is not the overriding concern.

5) "We want some of the action."
Communal rather than hierarchical.

5) The catechist is informed concerning the needs and religious expectations of those to be catechized. Catechesis is planned in such a way as to maximize participation by the total community. No "Lone Ranger" shows here.

6) "Everybody talkin' 'bout heaven ain't goin' there."
Praxis: catechesis leads us into action for justice. Action/reflection is the Church's model. Christian education must be informed and transformed by action. Action must not be hasty but rather shaped by careful reflection in community.

6) Mission for the Black church is reshaping the world according to God's justice. Mission is essential to catechesis. In our learning experiences, together we rededicate ourselves to the work yet to be done before the Lord's coming.

7) "God's not finished with us yet."
Process-oriented rather than static.

7) No form of catechesis is absolute. Christian life by its very nature is movement, change, pilgrimage—for such is God's action among his people.

8) "God's grace will run ahead of you . . ."
Charismatic: drawing forth the gifts of the Holy Spirit present in the community of believers. Demanding excellence in all dimensions of church life.

8) Community gathers around the charism of a minister of the Word, the catechist. However, it is imperative that the minister have personally experienced the overwhelming power of God's mystery and that he/she is free and willing to share this relationship with others.

9) "My soul's so happy I can't sit down!"
Immediacy of God's presence in the life of the believer. We can refer to this as realized eschatology. The *eschaton* has

9) Feeling the presence of the Spirit moving across the altar of your heart in real ways and not vicariously. God's presence is given expression in outward manifestations of shouting,

dawned. Black people reach into God's *eschaton* (endtime) and discover the Kingdom (God's rule) as here yet not here.	handclapping, foot-tapping, dancing, handwaving, etc. Learners are taught to reverence God's manifestations in their own lives and those of others.

Aesthetics and Catholic Catechetical Ministry

As Black people look at the experience of our past, reflect on the meanings of our present experience, and forge ahead toward unimagined futures—new images, symbols, myths, rites, and dances are created. By taking the raw data of our experience and translating it, shaping and reshaping it, the artist in each of us creates expressions which are profound statements of how we perceive those experiences.

In the art of Henry O. Tanner and Charles White, in the sculpture of Elizabeth Catlett, in the movement of Pearl Primus and Judith Jamison, in the melodious voice of Dinah Washington, in the music of Hubert Laws, in the poetry of Langston Hughes, and in the literary gifts of Jean Toomer, we possess the best possible definition of the Black aesthetic touching every fiber of Black existence. **Our bodies, our stories, and our dreams themselves are an eloquence.**

For catechists working with Catholics, *The National Catechetical Directory* offers several important directives which can be helpful in determining how the Black aesthetic connects with catechetical ministry.

> Human cultures also mirror divine attributes in various ways. The religions of humanity, especially, give a certain perception "of that hidden power which hovers over the course of things and over the events of human life, at times, indeed, recognition can be found of a Supreme Divinity and of a Supreme Father too. Such a perception and such a recognition instill the lives of these people with a profound religious sense." These are concrete examples and expressions of what can be termed God's natural revelation (#51).

> In liturgical celebrations, homogeneous cultural, racial, or ethnic communities have the right to use their own language and cultural expressions of faith in ritual, music, dance, and art. However, while diversity enriches the Church and makes it possible for the participants to experience worship more deeply, adaptations must respect the nature of liturgy as the worship of the Church. Not every cultural adaptation will be possible or suitable for liturgical use . . . (#137).

Again, in 1978 the American Bishops' Committee on the Liturgy published an important document, *Environment and Art in Catholic Worship*. In this statement the bishops have affirmed:

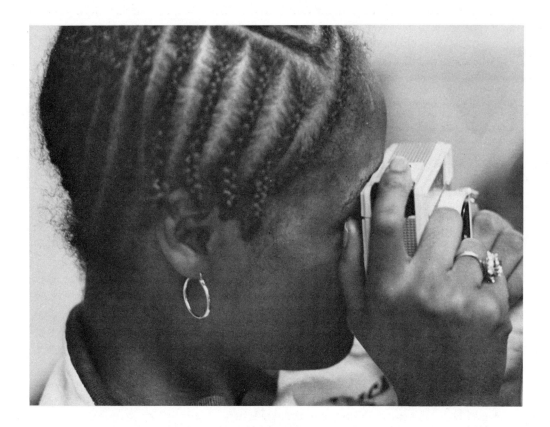

Every word, gesture, movement, object, appointment must be real in the sense that it is *our own* [emphasis added]. It must come from the deepest understanding of ourselves [not careless, phony, counterfeit, pretentious, exaggerated, etc.] (#14).

In another place the bishops have stated,

Because different cultural and subcultural groups in our society may have quite different styles of artistic expressions, one cannot demand any universal sacred forms (#18).

In order to enhance your catechetical ministry, you must heighten your appreciation of the Black aesthetic, the unity, variety, balance, harmony, and the connectedness to real life you discover so readily among Black folk. At the same time, you must be sensitive to the diversities among Blackamericans themselves. Like other peoples, our realities tend to differ somewhat given different conditions of time, place, or circumstance. Hence our perception of beauty will also differ.

Look at the colors, textures, juxtapositioning of the various elements, sizes, shapes, visions, concepts, values, attitudes, possibilities, strengths, and weaknesses of each art form relative to your catechetical purpose. Does that story, dance, gesture, art, symbol, media most clearly resonate with the truth of the people's lives? If not, perhaps you should search out a more appropriate artistic expression in dialogue with the learners themselves.

PRESENTATION B: Dale's Cone of Learning

An important teaching/learning principle to keep in mind when planning or designing Black church education experiences is:

> We remember 10 percent of what we HEAR.
> We remember 50 percent of what we SEE.
> We remember 90 percent of what we DO.

Reflecting on the insights of this proverbial statement, our teaching interest turns to "Dale's Cone of Learning."

Dale's Cone of Learning

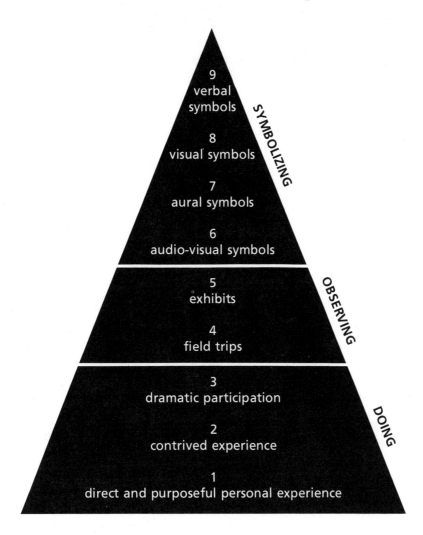

I have found "Dale's Cone of Learning" (herein adapted for our use) a helpful tool for evaluating teaching/learning methodology. It was developed by Edgar Dale, professor of education at Ohio State University. He has divided effective teaching/learning methods into three key categories:

Symbolizing   Observing   Doing

If you are interested in effective teaching, begin at the bottom of the cone and not at the top. The bottom of the cone (level 1) is the *most* effective teaching/learning method, while the top of the cone (level 9) is the *least* effective method of teaching, sharing faith.

Not surprisingly, words end up on the top, in the ninth and last position. Yet many catechists and pastoral ministers continue to act as though they were in first position. Lectures still dominate our teaching. Even the standard "aids"—maps, slides, cassettes—come in a low position.

Therefore, for your next teaching/learning experience, try to employ more **observing** and **doing** groups in your planning and teaching. Place the methods and resources at the bottom of Dale's Cone at the top of your personal use list.

Admittedly, Dale's Cone is not entirely applicable to catechetical ministry since ours is the sharing of a personal encounter, a tradition, and a community experience rather than simply teaching a subject such as math or reading. We are, in fact, communicating a living person, Christ Jesus. However, some of the principles and insights can enhance our catechesis.

Symbolizing

Level 9: Verbal Symbols—words

The old folk sing a song about "Everybody talkin' 'bout heaven ain't goin' there." These lyrics remind me of the endless number of lectures and homilies I have heard that not only reeked with boredom but raised within me definite questions concerning the sincerity of the messenger. Did the one who spoke actually have an emotional, gut-level experience of the message, or was the contact with the message strictly cerebral? Our elders sharply remind us that there are people—church folk included—who do a lot of verbalizing about theology and who deliver eloquent and polite elocutions about God, but who have never truly met God, walked with him, or talked with him. Their messages, as truthful as they might be, frequently do not touch the deepest core of people's lives. So their messages are void: talk, talk, talk.

Level 8: Visual Symbols—maps, charts, drawings, blackboards

The Brooklyn church where I once ministered was an environment filled with eye-catching murals, ikons, bright colors, and greenery. The changing seasonal banners, ceramic vessels, moveable furniture, bold vestments, and the gathered community itself were lively images of the Christian message. Everything and everyone seemed to contain an eloquence. The congregation's heritage, its pain and its glory, were clearly carved into the environment.

Environments for religious education should say something about the people who gather there and for what purpose they gather. Taking our cue from our wise grandparents, we must relearn how to take little and do much with it.

A bouquet of fresh flowers, a colorful poster, a bright tablecloth, and a well-chosen piece of sculpture or a painting go a long way in transforming a dull space into a warm one which communicates a sense of life and hospitality. When your lesson centers around a creation theme, an informal setting in a local park or yard will enhance your message. A message on family values might take place most effectively in a home. A session on building community might appropriately be held by sitting at a large, circular table in order to facilitate conversation and person-to-person contact—essential aspects of the message itself.

Simple line and stick-figure drawings have been helpful in my own teaching ministry, especially in settings where media resources are not budgeted or readily available. Such drawings are effective with all ages for several reasons:

- Drawings enable the catechist and the learning community to be on the same level with the same visual information available to both. This is quite important, especially in adult learning.
- Illustrations point to symbolic meanings. Without symbols our religious talk becomes simply theology and not catechetics.
- Positive images of ourselves and Black reality developed *by* Black people *for* Black people are a constitutive element in the catechesis of Black people.

Level 7: Aural Symbols—radio, phonograph, cassette recorder
A friend of mine once admitted that her inability to sing well limited her use of music in her teaching. However, she soon learned to play a record and teach her students to sing along.

It is frequently said in the Black church tradition that the Spirit does not descend without a song. With a wealth of Black sacred/secular music at our disposal today—through cassette tapes, radio broadcasts, and records—music should seldom be a missing ingredient in our catechesis or our liturgy.

For professional enrichment, catechists should take advantage of tape libraries featuring the talks of noted theologians and thinkers. Some adult religious-education experiences have focused on these tapes, followed by discussion.

Level 6: Audio-Visual Symbols—movies, slides, filmstrips, TV
The term *audio-visuals* probably generates some level of fear in many catechists. Questions abound: Do we have the best machinery? Do I know how to operate it? What if the machine breaks down? Such real questions can readily turn you off to the use of audio-visual resources in your teaching.

Audio-visuals, like all media, should aid in focusing the theme and the

teaching/learning objectives of your lesson. Audio-visual material should center the message more clearly, highlight an aspect of the message, or stimulate a deeper probing into the theme's meaning for daily living. Therefore, a good rule of thumb is that the underuse rather than the overuse of audio-visuals is a key to teaching success. With this perspective, many of the normal fears of audio-visual symbolizing will disappear.

Audio-visuals should be previewed before use in order to be sure that the program is not outdated, sentimental, or in poor physical condition and that it does fulfill the objectives of your learning experience. Previewing will enable you to know beforehand the uses and limitations of the media. Previewing also helps you determine the reactions you might expect from your learners.

Plan what you will do before and after viewing the audio-visual resource. If provided, review the discussion guide. A follow-up discussion frequently enables the participants to penetrate the theme by drawing out meanings for life.

A few audio-visual pointers:
- Be well prepared prior to your learning experience.
- Check the environment, seating arrangements, sound controls, lights, projector bulbs, and electrical outlets.
- Correctly position and cue your equipment—projector, screen, recorder, etc.—so that all things are ready to roll once you flip the switch.

Observing

Level 5: Exhibits—banners, church art, statues, dioramas
Many Blackamerican families encompass a variety of religious expressions and traditions. This is true within my own family. Some of the significant theological distinctions between the churches are often, I have found, exemplified in the architecture—its symbolism or lack of symbolism.

Generally, Protestant churches are austere and focus upon two key symbols: the pulpit and sometimes a bare cross. Symbolism beyond this is minimal.

Catholic and Orthodox churches are usually rich in symbolism with a focal emphasis on the altar-table and ambo (lectern/pulpit). Candles, flowers, ikons, and statues add symbolic richness to the environment.

These distinctions, though somewhat generalized (you will note that Black worship is invariably embellished by symbolic, ritual movements, uniforms, gestures, and protocol) reflect the diverse theological postures. In an article entitled "Are You Saved?" Rev. Halbert Weidner states that Catholic-Christians affirm that the sacred can be revealed in natural symbols; the material—such as water, bread, wine, human touch, oil, perfumings, and crafts—can evoke a religious response. Conversely, Protestant-Christians tend to equate the spiritual with the nonphysical, and thus the appeal to the eye is limited. This is not to say that there is no sense of beauty and order, but it tends to be austere and demanding. This approach to the physical is, no doubt, the most important distinguishing mark among Christians.

Christian tradition notwithstanding, Black churches must be places of beauty and color that communicate a sense of life. Regardless of a community's economic condition, the pastoral ministers and the people must be committed to a clean, orderly, attractive worshiping and learning space. Pictures should be framed, not taped to the wall. Flowers should be fresh; plants should be real, not artificial. Banners should be well designed, of artistic quality, and hung properly. Although these are seemingly small items of concern, when it comes to effective teaching/learning, substantiveness, simplicity, and meaning are of fundamental importance. As Dostoyevsky has one of his characters say, "The world will be saved by beauty."

Level 4: Field Trips—picnics, tours, retreats

In the summer months many churches provide opportunities for poor people to abandon the heat, monotony, and frustration of city life if only for a day in the country. Church buses quickly fill up as persons board with picnic baskets, coolers, baseball bats, and straw hats! It is certain that a large number of poor people would never get a chance to experience anything different from city life if the Black churches did not organize such outings.

Picnics, tours, camp meetings, pulpit exchanges, interchurch fellowship, and retreats offer new ventures of exploration for congregations while also serving an educational purpose. Exposure to new surroundings and people can give added motivation and challenge to the routine atmosphere and congregational life of your church and/or learning community.

Doing

Level 3: Dramatic Participation—plays, projects, puppets

Remember: if we do it, we know it. There is no substitute for active participation on the part of your learners.

A couple of years ago I was privileged to participate in a Black heritage eucharistic liturgy held at Holy Name Cathedral in Chicago. The overflowing crowd of school children and their teachers joined in the jubilant, victory celebration by handclapping, foot-stomping, handwaving, and spontaneous "Amen's"! However, to prepare for this celebration and set the tone for worship, just prior to the beginning of the liturgy, a group of mimers circled the altar-table and, in black leotards and white make-up, pantomimed the story of Sojourner Truth.*

I watched the reaction of the worshipers who were quickly absorbed

---

*Born a slave in 1797, Sojourner Truth rose to become an outspoken Black freedom fighter and advocate for women's rights. She was known as a "God-intoxicated woman." Originally named Isabella, she received a divinely inspired name reflective of her life's mission of liberation.

into the action and movement of the story. The mood for worship was created as everyone settled down and focused on the mimers' actions and experienced the power of this freedom fighter's story.

Your catechetical ministries can be greatly enriched through the creative use of drama, puppets, masks, and projects. Each of these expressions allows for individuals to explore alternative dimensions of their personalities, as well as grapple with life-circumstances and issues in a safe, healing environment in order to be guided toward Gospel-based solutions.

Many colleges have theater arts departments or mime troupes. Some churches are encouraging the gifts of "liturgical performers" who will enhance the worship through dance, movement, and mime. Scanning your local bookstores will give loads of references for the use of dramatic participation with adults, youth, and children.

Level 2: Contrived Experience—games, mock-ups, models

Most religious-education textbooks provide a wide variety of learning activities and games which highlight certain aspects of a lesson. Do not allow your teaching, however, to be limited by these suggestions. Learn how to "make do" and create original activities.

It is interesting to note that while America's parents give their money to Mattel, parents in the Third World teach their children to create games out of the stuff of everyday life: rocks, soil, sticks, scrap materials. Creating a game involves imagination and that, too, is an essential tool for learning and religious experience.

Level 1: Direct and Purposeful Personal Experience

When we share with others the plan of God unfolding in our lives, our faith is celebrated and the faith of others is strengthened. A person struggling with a chemical dependency can be encouraged to seek professional guidance through the sincere testimony of a fellow believer. There's nothing like a testimony thread from the heart of someone who has walked through dangers seen and unseen to spark a lively response among most believers. When we are most in touch with our deepest selves and express our innermost being, we often discover that we are not alone: others are thinking and feeling the same things.

Opportunities for storytelling and storysharing should be an element of each learning experience. Ask your learners for instances in their own lives that confirm the perspectives the lesson is pointing up. Share your personal life-journey. Elders in every community stand as living witnesses that our possibilities reach higher than the reality we face. Church and community leaders who have given their hands to struggle possess numerous life-experiences and insights which, if invited, can enrich your teaching supported by the testimony of people's lives.

PRESENTATION C: Optimum Catechetical Experiences for the Black Community

The following sections will stress and highlight some of the primary ways Black people learn. Each illustration emphasizes learning techniques that prioritize personal, active engagement (as suggested by level 1 of "Dale's Cone of Learning") and that integrate the significant aspects of Black aesthetics. Applying insights from these two fields—learning theory and aesthetics—allows us to fashion optimum catechetical experiences for the Black community.

An Aural People

Father Clarence Rivers, a premier Blackamerican Catholic voice advocating Black traditional worship styles in Catholic liturgy, has identified the ocular versus aural cultural traditions. Rivers points out that Western culture is primarily ocular, that is, of the eye. "It tends to comprehend the world through the bias of the sense of sight, a bias that is somehow connected with a book-oriented culture in which sight dominates and mutes the other senses." On the other hand, Rivers points out that biblical peoples, along with Black peoples, are primarily from oral-aural traditions. Such peoples value the poetic over and above the conceptual, and personal involvement over analytical detachment.

Examine your educational ministries. I might predict that you will discover that your catechesis as well as your parish liturgy is "Western" with a vengeance.

With cultural roots in Afrika, Blackamericans are steeped in an aural cultural tradition. This phenomenon is given expression in the fact that, for the most part, Black people are an oral people. Black folk learn best through such media as storytelling, art, drama, and music. Blacks communicate best through movement, gesture, ritual, prayer, humor, testifying, sermons, and so forth.

But affirming the dominance of the oral-aural tradition in Black life does not, in any way, diminish the necessity of Afrikan-Americans being fully equipped for Western living through a capacity to read well and to write and think analytically. Rather, what this affirmation states is that when catechists or preachers are planning curriculum designs (or even sermons), they must seriously take into account the key ways in which Black adults, youth, and children learn and employ these methods for the effective communication of the message of faith.

Music

Afrikans have historically communicated through music ("the talking drums") and movement to share news, to put the departed to rest, to name the newborn, as well as to celebrate times and seasons. Music celebrated the marrying of lovers and the healing of broken, weary spirits. Music invades Black life at every dimension of our existence.

Afrikan-Americans, like other Americans, find themselves in a country very different from that of their ancestors. Because of a profound love for life, Blackamericans have made music and magic with their voices, their hands, and their feet. Black folk would rather sing than weep—like any other of the world's peoples. Had Blacks not been able to make music, they would have perished.

Our music can be heard in our street sounds, laughter, tears, hymns, chants, prayers, sermons, jazz, and our Saturday night "jamming." As the poet and social critic Haki R. Madhubuti writes, "All Black people do not play musical instruments / but all Black people are musicians."

Music, like all of life, is profoundly political, and Blackamericans have long been aware of this vital property. We have come to appreciate how music was used as a weapon of deception by slaves. Lerone Bennett, Jr., has written in *The Shaping of Black America,* "Slaves . . . used music as a medium of communication. The cries and hollers and field calls contained secret messages and code words. In truth, double meanings permeated the whole fabric of this music. One song, for example, used Jesus' name to mask an open and obvious invitation to the slaves to steal away to freedom. 'Steal away, steal away to Jesus. Steal away, steal away home. I ain't got long to stay here.' "

As an oral-aural people, music is woven into the fabric of the dailiness of Black life. Everywhere there thrive melodies, tunes, jazz rhythms, blues, and the spirituals. Listen at the door of storefronts and church basements and you will hear upbeat Gospel sounds, foot-tapping, finger-popping, and pulsating rhythm and blues.

Ask your learners: "What music, which songs have a religious significance to *you?*" Sounds, lyrics, tempos, and rhythms you never associated with a so-called God-consciousness are frequently viewed by others in quite the opposite manner. Popular songs concerning human love, made and broken covenants, or street life can forcibly reveal the values (or disvalues), political quest, religious search, turmoil, ecstacy, and questions of a people.

Dr. James H. Cone, America's foremost Black theologian, states in *The Spirituals and the Blues* that both the sacred and secular music from the Black experience boldly lift up and magnify theological themes. **Black music undeniably reflects how God has moved and is moving among Black folk of faith.**

Catechesis and liturgy experienced in the Black community must draw from these sources rich with the spiritual yearnings of a people. *The National Catechetical Directory* affirms this for Catholic catechists when it states:

> The language of the particular group should be used in the catechesis of its members; not just its vocabulary, but its thought

patterns, cultural idioms, customs, and symbols. Catechetical materials should suit its characteristics and needs. Rather than simply translating or adapting material prepared for others, it is generally necessary to develop new materials (#194).

The giftedness of a Mahalia Jackson, Billie Holliday, John Coltrane, James Cleveland, Gertrude "Ma" Rainey, Edwin and Walter Hawkins, Commodores, Emotions, Stevie Wonder, or Gil Scott-Heron has an important place in the faith-formation of Black Catholic-Christians. Each musician and musical style bears a message that can speak to Black hearts something of the goodness of life and the hope to which we are all called.

A creative catechist can take even a negative popular tune—for instance, on the sexual exploitation of women—and through a process of critical dialogue and biblical reflection on the nature and role of women, guide the learners to a fuller appreciation of the honorable manner in which Christian faith looks upon women.

Attentiveness to the people with whom you minister will call your attention to the music that touches them most deeply.

Ritual

Ntozake Shange's choreopoem, *for colored girls who have considered suicide / when the rainbow is enuf,* is a Black woman's creative statement about the journeys of her sisters, their painful contours, as she seeks to envision new Black women moving together to "the ends of their own rainbows."

It is interesting that at a highpoint in the story's action, one of the women, filled with anguish, cries out for something to make her whole again. One woman proposes a laying on of hands. This ritual action, rooted in the primal power of human touch and the New Testament notion of healing, is a communal celebration of calling down the powers larger than self to make this woman whole once more and again. Together the women affirm the hurting woman and minister to her pain and support her healing.

Traditionally, Afrikan peoples have celebrated these and other of life's key moments. Ritual has provided a language and symbols to celebrate the passage of time and seasons. Birth, naming, maturity, marriage, sickness, healing, and death are celebrated by the whole people through song, story, symbol, dance, ceremonial foods, blessings, and prayers.

Theologian Monika Hellwig, in a book entitled *Tradition: The Catholic Story Today,* connects cultural and religious rituals, describing the connections between the Christian pattern of worship and that of Israel as being deeply rooted in a natural, cultural response.

> Our basic pattern of worship, like that of Israel, is a celebration; we recall a past event, making it present again by our participation in it. We contemplate such an event and meditate on the meaning of it, seeing it clearly in retrospect as a wonderful act of

God. From looking at it in the past, we learn to discern the wonderful acts of God in our present world and to know what is the invitation of God into the future. For us, the classic event is the Paschal Mystery of the death and Resurrection of Christ, which we celebrate explicitly in the Eucharist, to which all the other sacraments and celebrations are closely linked.

Ritual is integrated into the life of the Black church. In its preaching, ushers, church nurses, deacons, banquets, altar calls, and protocol, the Black personality experiences the specialness of the "holy" *(mysterium tremendum),* the encounter with God.

Plan celebrations around your learner's focal life-moments, such as births, conversion-experiences, sacramental encounters, graduations, achievements, heritage, retirements, and life-stages which can be creatively and meaningfully ritualized in the context of your church or educational setting.

This writer has been inspired to develop several ritual celebrations for the Black Catholic community. However, my own work has been inspired and propelled by the premier efforts of Edward Sims, Jr., of Philadelphia, author of the "Black Family Ritual Series." Professor Sims has designed five family-community-centered rituals around the following teachable moments: birth-naming, passage into adulthood, marriage, thanksgiving, and death.

Recovering ritual in Afrikan life, Jewish tradition, or uncovering the creative gifts of your learners themselves will enable your catechesis to reflect cultural realities and celebrate religious roots. Vatican II's *Decree on the Liturgy* gives us catechists in the Catholic tradition the encouragement to unearth and create those languages that speak to the reality of our experience.

> Even in the liturgy, the Church has no wish to impose a rigid uniformity in matters which do not involve the faith or the good of the whole community. Rather she respects and fosters the spiritual adornments and gifts of the various races and peoples. Sometimes, in fact, she admits such things into the liturgy itself, as long as they harmonize with its true and authentic spirit.

The Black Family in Ritual, Story, and Celebration

Black folk have historically devised ways of arresting the catastrophic effects of racism through a variety of unique social systems, lifestyles, and rituals often born in America but shaped by Afrikan cultural patterns.

At a time when family and relationships are at their lowest ebb in the Black community, as well as in the larger community, we are experiencing a revival of interest in the family reunion, family roots, heritage, and the preservation of memories about ourselves and our people.

By coming together as a family, the stories and memories of the family and the race are shared and passed on. While we sit around the feasting table and share the humorous and seemingly incredible tales of long-deceased relatives, jack-leg preachers, lost loves, and so forth, we are, in effect, preserving these beautiful memories of our best selves. We join the voices of our ancestors singing, "Will the circle be unbroken?"

The poet Carolyn Rodgers draws together these elements of family bonds, rootedness, and elder-reverence in a poem entitled, "It Is Deep (don't never forget the bridge that you crossed over on)." With finely honed perception and artistic skill, she writes of her mother:

> My mother, religious-negro, proud of
> having waded through a storm, is very obviously
> a sturdy Black bridge that I
> crossed over, on.

Through sharing family memories, family celebrations, and rituals we come to know our family members more intimately, where they came from and how they endured. In other words, family gatherings are that "blest tie that binds."

Similarly, Alex Haley's *Roots* is concerned with a "family reunion" distanced and dispersed by history. Haley's search for identity grew out of an informal story that had been repeated generation after generation and told to him.

Do you recall the emotionally charged scene in the Afrikan village where Haley's account of his ancestor, Kunta Kinte, was confirmed by the *griot*, the storyteller of the community? For Haley the old, old Story came alive with a new power as he was embraced by his Afrikan family in an ancient, human ritual of acceptance, solidarity, and communion.

Family reunions, storytelling, rituals, celebrations, prayers, hymns, testifying, humor, and "tabletalk" are some of the primary ways a people's heritage and insight are preserved and passed on to future generations. These folk expressions are primarily aesthetic expressions; they are also important learning experiences.

Action: Witness-in-Deed

Persons learn best when they are actively engaged in doing. One church with which this author is familiar decided to compose a letter to its congressperson protesting the proposed federal budget cuts for social services to the poor and elderly. This particular action occurred during the Sunday Eucharist. Consistent with the biblical prophetic tradition, this worshiping community responded to the Word that Sunday in a collective manner. At the conclusion of the Sunday celebration, several persons were publicly blessed and commissioned to go to Washington, D.C., bearing this "living word" requesting that justice have a hearing.

What a marvelous and dramatic expression of a Christian community's faith and solidarity with its brothers and sisters. This particular church structured an opportunity into its highest moment of celebration and assembly in order to listen to the unadulterated Word of God and respond through active, concrete engagement to real human need.

When was the last time your church registered a protest against any issue impacting upon human life? How frequently do you engage your learners in a critical reflection of their environment, their people, their world community, or themselves?

Letter writing is a solitary expression, while there exist numerous ways to enable Christians to express their owned faith through loving service in the world because of Jesus. There are elders to be visited, family relationships to be healed, neighborhoods to be beautified, and minds to be elevated.

Persons

The best teaching/learning resources are persons in your church, educational setting, or larger community. Storytellers, carpenters, singers, artists, and leaders of prayer are undoubtedly as plentiful in your community as they are in mine. Normally, it simply requires an honest request for a person's services. "We have seen how effectively you reach out to the sick and shut-in. Would you share some of your experiences with others and join our outreach team?"

> In order to ensure that false images and myths are not perpetuated and that paternalism is avoided, we must bring people from the Third World into the preparation of material so that they are co-responsible partners in our education. Their insights and experiences should help to ensure that the material has the correct perspective and is sensitive to the sense of dignity and self-respect which people in the Third World have towards nation-building and development.
>
> World Council of Churches,
> *Development Education,* Geneva, 1969

Presently in the majority of Black Catholic settings, the master catechists are non-Black. Practically speaking, these non-Black clergy, religious, laity, and catechists ministering in a Black cultural context are "missionaries," in the richest biblical sense. These missionaries are sent forth to preach and teach the Word, to build up the Church, to form indigenous leaders, and then to press on to new frontiers where the Church is not yet established. *The National Catechetical Directory* points out that "ideally the catechist will be a member of the particular racial, cultural, or ethnic group. Catechists who are not members of the group should understand and empathize with it, besides having adequate catechetical formation" (#194). Therefore, the non-Black minister of the Word must engage the talents and gifts of a wide number of Black people for the effective communication of the message.

The Black catechist, or minister of the Word, must also depend on the invaluable gift of other Black people, especially the elders, struggling single

parents, successful Black men and women, perceptive and refreshing Black thinkers.

Think of your educational ministry in terms of creating optimum catechetical experiences for the Black community by drawing on the strengths and resources inherent in Black culture. As we have shown, we can integrate Black aesthetics (music, storytelling, etc.) with sound teaching/learning principles (such as "Dale's Cone of Learning") for effective Black catechesis.

The following chapters are intended to assist you and your catechist formation group to appreciate (1) the role of Jesus as teacher in relation to the historic role of the Black preacher, (2) the Afrikan storytelling tradition, and (3) the strategies necessary to deepen and intensify your teaching ministry.

INTEGRATION

A story is told about Michelangelo's pushing a huge piece of rock down a street. A curious neighbor sitting lazily on the porch of his house called

Personal Responses

1) Closing my eyes and focusing on my learners, I can see their beauty reflected in . . .

2) If I were to identify the aspects of my local community that are the *least* compelling and beautiful, these would be . . .

3) I feel I participate in the distressing aspects of my environment in the following ways . . .

4) The stories, folkways, wisdom, or creative expressions of Black people I personally find most inspiring are . . .

TEACHING / LEARNING RESOURCES

BOOKS

Bishops' Committee on the Liturgy. *Environment and Art in Catholic Worship.* Washington, DC: United States Catholic Conference, 1978.

Capacchione, Lucia. *The Creative Journal: The Art of Finding Yourself.* Chicago: Swallow Press, 1979.

Durka, Gloria and Smith, Joanmarie, ed. *Aesthetic Dimensions of Religious Education.* New York: Paulist Press, 1978.

Foley, Rita Walsh. *Let's Create!* Huntington, IN: Our Sunday Visitor, 1974.

Furnish, Dorothy J. *Exploring the Bible with Children.* Nashville: Abingdon Press, 1975.

Huck, Gabe. *A Book of Family Prayer.* New York: Seabury Press, 1979.

O'Connor, Elizabeth. *Eighth Day of Creation.* Waco, TX: Word Books, 1971.

Rivers, Clarence J. *The Spirit in Worship.* Cincinnati: Stimuli, 1978.

Sims, Edward. *Black Family Rituals.* P.O. Box 4956, Philadelphia, PA 19119.

PERIODICALS

Blackguard: Resources for Multi-cultural Christian Education. National Council of Churches, 475 Riverside Drive, 7th Floor, New York City, NY 10027.

JED Share. Joint Educational Development, 287 Park Avenue South, New York City, NY 10010. Subscription: $5.50 annually.

Mass Media Newsletter. 2116 North Charles Street, Baltimore, MD 21218. Subscription: $12 annually.

Media and Values. National Sisters' Communications Service, 1962 South Shenandoah, Los Angeles, CA 90034. Subscription: $10 annually.

New Catholic World. Special Issue on Art and Belief. January/February 1980. Ramsey, NJ: Paulist Press. $1.50 per copy.

MEDIA

"Nguzo Saba Films." (Afrikan and Third World folklore for children and all ages) 16mm story films. Distributed by: Beacon Films, P.O. Box 575, Norwood, MA 02062.

"Sweet Honey in the Rock." (Black women's singing group) Two albums. Available from: Redwood Records, P.O. Box 996, Ukiah, CA 95482.

"Using Media." (For Effective Audio-Visual Communications) Series of ten filmstrips with records or cassettes and guide book. Roa Films, 1696 North Astor Street, Milwaukee, WI 53202.

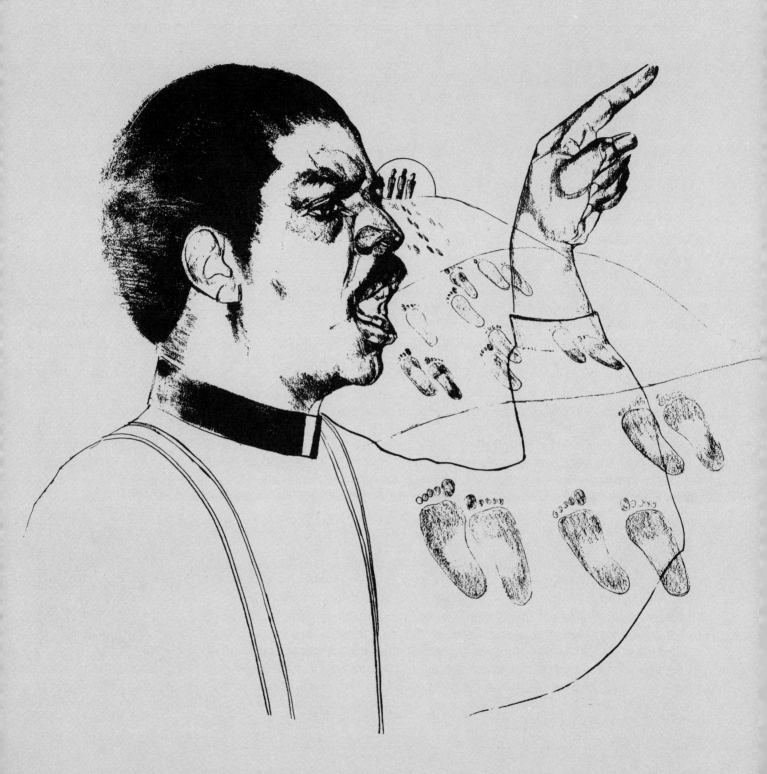

3
Jesus as Teacher and the Black Preacher

Jesus the teacher presents a model for Black catechesis. The Black preacher stands as another model for our teaching ministry. Both of these sources are historical and contemporary and possess the power to inform our tasks as catechists.

When one of you says, "I am with Paul," and another, "I am with Apollos"—aren't you acting like worldly men? After all, who is Apollos? And who is Paul? We are simply God's servants, by whom you were led to believe. Each one of us does the work the Lord gave him to do: I planted the seed, Apollos watered the plant, but it was God who made the plant grow. The one who plants and the one who waters really do not matter. It is God who matters, for he makes the plant grow. There is no difference between the man who plants and the man who waters; God will reward each one according to the work he has done. For we are partners working together for God, and you are God's field.

1 Corinthians 3:4-9

The Black preacher appeared early on the plantation and found his function as the healer of the sick, the interpreter of the unknown, the comforter of the sorrowing, the supernatural avenger of wrong, and the one who rudely but picturesquely expressed the longing, disappointment, and resentment of a stolen and oppressed people.

Dr. W. E. B. DuBois,
The Souls of Black Folk

This learning experience aims to enable you:

TO KNOW	To equip catechists with a fuller appreciation of the message and methods of Jesus the teacher.
TO FEEL	To enable catechists to experience the catechetical implications of the Black preaching-event.
TO DO	To be capable of retelling the biblical story, drawing on the language, symbols, and word-pictures of Black folk of faith.

Turn to the "Personal Responses" on page 67.

Turn to the "Personal Responses" on page 67.

INITIATION: Remembering

Moments That Move Us to Testify

Go alone to a quiet place with only this book at hand and a sheet of paper and a pen.

Sit quietly, close your eyes, and take at least three slow, deep breaths. Get a sense of yourself being on a life-journey. Notice the kind of path that has been yours and notice how you have traveled that path.

Become aware of your significant life-moments as an adult. Focus on a memorable moment when you encountered God in a way you can never forget. Get in touch with this key life-moment. Pay close attention to the experience and your response to it. Take the time you need to look at this special experience from every possible side.

Now bring to memory the most important persons who have nurtured your relationship with the Lord along your journey. Let that person—or persons—come into your imagination and communicate your gratefulness to them. Thank the Lord for the wonderful gift of his presence in the way you are moved to do so at this time. When you feel ready, open your eyes.

On the sheet of paper, make some jottings to yourself using either simple illustrations, a few lines of poetry, a doodle, or a symbol which best permits you to express the inner dialogue you just experienced. You may have focused on a nature walk, a celebration, a charitable deed, or the birth of a baby. Whatever images or word-pictures came across the "altar of your heart" during the remembering meditation, decide which you would like to share with others and jot these down.

Below are some questions that might be helpful to you as you proceed.

1) In good times (or in times of distress) what biblical story, image, or prayer comes most readily to mind?

2) What is "your song"? When do you find yourself turning to this song? What memories do you associate with this melody?

3) Are there particular persons who have entered your life at special times and have left an imprint on your pilgrim journey?

Black Preachers and Their Message

Listen to a tape, film, filmstrip, videotape, or recording of a Black preacher in his/her pulpit. Or tune in to a church service on the local radio. **Our contention is that the Christian educator has much to learn from the traditional styles and principles of the Black preacher.** Carefully listen to the preacher. Now respond to the following:

What is unique about the style?

language?

imagery?

theology?

Jot down what elements of presence and presentation most dramatically touched you. What story? What symbols? What movements stirred you or captured your imagination or attention most of all?

PRESENTATION

Journeying with Jesus

Let us look at how Jesus himself taught and shared faith. There are many New Testament examples we could draw from, but the story of the walk along the road to Emmaus (Luke 24:13-35) is a fitting illustration.

Jesus joins the journey of the disciples (verses 15-17) • By walking with his folk, he was enabled to understand and hear them. Jesus is not afraid to ask questions about their reality.

> As the two men talked and discussed, Jesus himself drew near and walked along with them; they saw him, but somehow did not recognize him. Jesus said to them, "What are you talking about back and forth, as you walk along?"

By walking with your community, you will be enabled to understand and hear them. Talk *with* them instead of merely showing up to teach and preach. Let the people see you in other life situations. Relax, have a cup of tea, and talk with them about *their* life concerns.

Jesus evokes the fears, discouragements, heartaches, and heartbreaks of his disciples (verses 19-24) • The disciples expected Jesus to be a political revolutionary and, perhaps, situate them nicely with "new homes" and "Cadillacs"!

> "What things [have been happening in Jerusalem the last few days]?" Jesus asked.
>
> "The things that happened to Jesus of Nazareth," they answered. "This man was a prophet and was considered by God and by all the people to be mighty in words and deeds. Our chief priests and rulers handed him over to be sentenced to death, and he was nailed to the cross. And we had hoped that he would be the one who was going to redeem Israel! Besides all that, this is now the third day since it happened. Some of the women of our group surprised us; they went at dawn to the grave but could not find his body. They came back saying they had seen a vision of angels who told them that he is alive. Some of our group went to the grave and found it exactly as the women had said; but they did not see him."

Avoid approaching your people with an agenda; put your books down and learn the value of listening. Your agenda, plans, and programs must wait until the cries of their hearts and lives are expressed. Among Black people I believe this listening to be best exercised not through detached, scientific, or sociological instruments but rather through one-to-one, personal, human contact.

Jesus retells the old, old Story of God's faithfulness to enable his disciples to grapple with their inner pain with a new strength (verses 25-26) • By having truly listened to the disciples' plea for help, Jesus was equipped to offer them the clarity of the biblical testimony.

> Then Jesus said to them, "How foolish you are, how slow you are to believe everything the prophets said! Was it not necessary for the Messiah to suffer these things and enter his glory?"

Jesus listened in a manner that enabled the disciples to speak their minds and hearts freely. But after he listened, he offered them a direction for life.

He shared with the disciples their link in history to their ancestors, to Moses, and to the prophets. They were not alone in their feelings of exile and abandonment. Truly, their ancestors had gone before them facing similar human needs. Jesus enabled his disciples to see in their religious history *their* story right now. As a catechist, can you illumine the present strife of Black people with the life-giving symbols of the Church community and the Black community?

There is no separate, discrete, neat, and stained-glass world of religious meaning distinct from the world of bunions, bulges, babies, and bills to which Christian education addresses itself. No! In the midst of incipient cultural strife and the dailiness of our lives, there is a hint of Good News. Catechesis brings the power and meaning of the symbols of our faith community to bear on the realities of Black life.

Jesus demonstrates his relationship to the community of Israel (verse 27) • Jesus pointed out how the recent events in Jerusalem were not isolated occurrences but were intimately related to the total sweep of Israel's long history.

> And Jesus explained to them what was said about him in all the Scriptures, beginning with the books of Moses and the writings of all the prophets.

The disappointment of the disciples was not unconnected to history. It was an intimate aspect of it, and Jesus demonstrated this when he shared how the Messiah must die so that he would rise again. Catechists must connect the Black story of joy, travail, and the struggle for deliverance with God's continuing Story.

Have not Blackamericans always identified with Israel? Didn't we speak about Egyptland and Babylon as paradigms of America? Didn't we speak of Israel and Canaanland as our people progressing toward freedom? Didn't we manifest these folk beliefs in our prayers, sermons, songs, blues, and jazz? Can our catechesis so inspire the present generation?

Jesus requests to share a hospitality meal with his disciples (verses 28-35) ● At this simple friendship meal, the eyes of the disciples were opened to recognize the Lord. This experience revealed a newly acquired understanding of Jesus' message and mission. Therefore, the joy could not be contained, and the disciples went at once to tell the others. Such a new understanding of the Lord's presence leads us, likewise, into service.

> They came near the village to which they were going, and Jesus acted as if he were going farther; but they held back, saying, "Stay with us; the day is almost over and it is getting dark." So he went in to stay with them. He sat at table with them, took the bread, and said the blessing; then he gave it to them. Their eyes were opened and they recognized him; but he disappeared from their sight. They said to each other, "Wasn't it like a fire burning in us when he talked to us on the road and explained the Scriptures to us?"
>
> They got up at once and went back to Jerusalem, where they found the eleven disciples gathered together with the others and saying, "The Lord is risen indeed! He has appeared to Simon!"
>
> The two of them explained to them what had happened on the road, and how they had recognized the Lord when he broke the bread.

Have you ever considered the fact that the most important feature of a family meal—table-fellowship—is not so much the food itself as it is the *sharing of the meal?* Sharing favorite dishes, stories of the goings-on in our lives, and prayer are the actions which make the meal a very human act.

Questions for Personal and Group Reflection
Take a serious look at your teaching, preaching, or witnessing. *In what ways do you reflect Jesus the model teacher? Are you truly present to the people? Are you fully attentive? Do you share authentically the total Gospel? What is your participation in the life of the local church and in worship and service?*

Fannie Lou as Teacher

Black history is rich with "teachers" in our homes, churches, schools, and larger community. Catechists should be encouraged to find examples of such teachers in Black history to share with their community. Fannie Lou Hamer is one such example.

Fannie Lou Hamer (October 6, 1917-March 14, 1977) stands out as a "**she**ro" of Black people, a living embodiment of these teaching principles. A poor, Mississippi sharecropper with little formal education, Fannie Lou rose as an outstanding spokesperson for other poor people denied human rights by White social structures.

In spite of physical debilities, she boldly struggled to change the labor and political conditions of her people through organized movements of protest and economic development.

Backed by her Christian faith, which exercised a great influence in her life, and by a profound sense of self-respect, Mrs. Hamer fought tirelessly in the face of numerous assaults, jailings, threats, and untold opposition. Ultimately, her unswerving and fearless commitment to justice won victories for her people. Her message of dignity, Black pride, economic self-help, and interdependence was heard and freely accepted by her fellow sharecroppers because she shared their condition—its pain and its gain.

"But That's Not Me . . ."

You may have come to a point when many real questions, fears, and anxieties are surfacing. You are perhaps a little nervous and apprehensive about "letting go" and being affective (as well as more effective) in your teaching. You protest saying, "It's not me. This would be just acting. My cultural experience is different. This shouting, demonstrating, and expressing is just not *me*!"

Whoever you are, these questions and related ones might be real for you and cannot be lightly dismissed. Serious catechetical ministry in the Black church must prompt you to reconsider and resolve these questions.

My response to these concerns is fourfold. First of all, be yourself. Persons accept you for being your most authentic self.

Secondly, and somewhat conversely, I would insist that if you are serious about the communication of the faith in the Black church, you must learn how to free yourself up a little bit. Loosen the fetters of your past socialization, ordering, and formation which restrict your emotional responses. Allow yourself to be taught by the religious impulses of Black folk where you minister.

Thirdly, it is not necessary to force the feeling. Respond to what *you* feel. Clearly, it is not possible to enter emotionally into the religious experience of others at every single moment. For instance, if someone is bodily and emotionally caught up in worship, but you are left cold—that might well be okay. However, you *must* grow to the capacity to appreciate and reverence the source of these expressions whatever they might be.

Above all, remember you are a guide to the goal, not the goal itself. You are not the message; you are a messenger.

INTEGRATION

Summarily, the mission and ministry of the Black preacher have been best expressed in the ways that are listed below.

> 1) **The preacher and the people share a close identity.** The preacher had his roots among the people and therefore was more quickly capable of establishing an intimacy of feeling with the folk.
> 2) **The preacher shares an experience of faith.** The preacher shares in the fortunes, struggles, and strides of the people. The preacher is in a right relationship with God.
> 3) **The preacher is able to talk the people's talk.** An ex-slave once said: "That ol' white preachin' wasn't nuthin' . . . ol' white preacher used to talk with his tongue without sayin' nuthin', but Jesus told us slaves to talk with our hearts."
> The preacher freely employs familiar language, images, symbols, and humor. The preacher's delivery is imaginative in style, using sweeping gestures, bodily movement, improvisation, and spontaneity.
> 4) **The preacher is involved with the worshiping congregation, bodily and emotionally.** This freedom takes place within a

> welcoming, receptive community. The congregation is free to respond because the preacher is free.
> 5) **The biblical story itself enables the preacher to interpret God's saving Word in the light of the lived experiences, struggles, and strides of the people.** The preaching-event is a poetic happening. It is tremendously earthbound, connected to the dailiness of Black lives.

For this INTEGRATION activity, it is suggested that the master catechist create an environment conducive to reflection. A tape of soft, instrumental music and the invitation to the participants to feel free to move around the room go a long way.

Questions for Personal and Group Reflection
How does the descriptive profile provided above reflect your own teaching? What are three ways this profile can reshape your teaching ministry?

Following this period for reflecting on your deepest feelings, a further enriching exercise might be coming together in small groups (perhaps triads) and sharing testimonies with each other.

You could conclude this activity by proclaiming a quote from the Scriptures such as the following:

> Like a mother feeding and looking
> after her own children,
> we felt so devoted and protective
> towards you, and had come to love you
> so much, that we were eager
> to hand over to you not only the
> Good News
> but our whole lives as well.
>
> 1 Thessalonians 2:8

CELEBRATION: I Love to Tell the Story

Environment: A scriptural shrine is central in the worship space. A candle is reverently lit. Incense is burned. Fresh flowers add brightness. All are seated in a traditional, Afrikan prayer circle.

Order of Service:

> When He calls me, I will answer.
> When He calls me, I will answer.
> When He calls me, I will answer.
> I'll be somewhere listenin' for my name.

I'll be somewhere listenin',
I'll be somewhere listenin',
I'll be somewhere listenin' for my name.

I'll be somewhere listenin',
I'll be somewhere listenin',
I'll be somewhere listenin' for my name.

A prayer is lifted up by someone moved by the Spirit.

Excerpts are read from a Black sermon, or a prayer is read from one of the resources mentioned in the TEACHING / LEARNING RESOURCES section of this chapter (see p. 68). Time is allotted for testimonies regarding the personal significance of this learning experience.

Conclude with the laying on of hands. Turn to your neighbor and place your hands on their shoulders and pray a simple blessing over them. Allow yourself the privilege of having the other person pray a blessing over you also. Then join together in singing the refrain of the traditional hymn, "I Love to Tell the Story."

I love to tell the Story;
'Twill be my theme in glory,
To tell the old, old Story
of Jesus and his love.

RESPONSE: Teaching as Jesus Did

To teach as Jesus did is an experience of liberation: bidding persons to live and inviting them to grow.

Father Henri Nouwen clearly states in his book, *Creative Ministry,* that "education is not primarily ministry because of what is taught but because of the nature of the educational process itself. Perhaps we have paid too much attention to the content of teaching without realizing that the teaching relationship is the most important factor in the ministry of teaching."

Jesus got radically involved in the lives of his people. When his people experienced the oppressive arm of the Roman conquerors, he too felt the same blows. By total identification with his people, Jesus was empowered to offer a life-transforming Word of love to a weary and fragmented nation.

The independent Black church gave birth to the Black preacher who, like the Afrikan storyteller and Jesus, was bonded to his people's present-day and historic struggles. It was largely due to the preacher's capacity to walk with his people that his spoken word was endowed with power to sustain and transform lives.

Catechists and other teaching ministers within today's Black Catholic communities have rich traditions from which to draw direction. Concern with catechetical content and methodology is key, but both the teaching ministries of Jesus and of the Black preacher demonstrate the fundamental importance of the *intimate relationship* between the catechist and the people. Involvement in people's lives will shape your message, inform its content, direct its delivery, and challenge its style.

Through all of this and in a most beautiful and lasting way, the people will come to know Jesus in the breaking of the Bread and in the Word. They will come to know the power of his resurrected life among them.

Personal Responses

1) As a minister of God's Word, I can imagine myself functioning most creatively and comfortably among my learners at times when . . .

2) My most fearsome inner/outer battle to improve my teaching style is . . .

3) I have been told that my admirable qualities and gifts as a catechist are . . .

4) My understanding of Jesus as a model teacher has deeply challenged me to . . .

TEACHING / LEARNING RESOURCES

BOOKS

Carter, Harold. *The Prayer Tradition of Black People.* Valley Forge, PA: Judson Press, 1976.

DuBois, W. E. B. *The Souls of Black Folk.* New York: Fawcett, 1968.

Johnson, James Weldon. *God's Trombones.* New York: Penguin Books, 1955.

Jordan, Clarence. *The Cotton Patch Version of Luke and Acts.* Chicago: Follett, 1969.

_____. *The Cotton Patch Version of Matthew and John.* Chicago: Follett, 1970.

_____. *The Cotton Patch Version of Paul's Epistles.* Chicago: Follett, 1968.

Mitchell, Henry H. *Black Preaching.* Philadelphia: Lippincott, 1970.

Roberts, J. Deotis. *Roots of a Black Future: Family and Church.* Philadelphia: The Westminster Press, 1980.

Shea, John. *Stories of God.* Chicago: The Thomas More Publishers, 1980.

Taylor, Gardner C. *How Shall They Preach.* Progressive Baptist Publishing House (850 North Grove Avenue, Elgin, IL 60120), 1977.

Thomas, Latta. *Biblical Faith and the Black American.* Valley Forge, PA: Judson Press, 1976.

ARTICLES

Mead, Margaret. "Celebration: A Human Need." *Catechist,* May 1976.

Religious Education. Special Issue on Spirituality and Religious Education. July-August 1980.

"Toward a New Introduction to Christian Theology: Telling the Story." *The Journal of the Interdenominational Theological Center,* Spring 1976.

MEDIA

"Black Religion II / The Black Preacher," (Black Culture Series). Filmstrip with record or cassette. Scholastic Book Services, 904 Sylvan Avenue, Englewood Cliffs, NJ 07632.

Hamer, Fannie Lou. "Songs My Mother Taught Me." Cassette tape, $5.00. Available from: Program in Black American Culture, Smithsonian Institute, Washington, DC 20506.

4
The Teaching Minister as Griot

Catechists are ministers of the Word and servants of the community. Their calling can be likened to the ancient Afrikan tradition of the *griot* and finds contemporary expression in the old folk among us.

Take care and be earnestly on your guard not to forget the things which your own eyes have seen, nor let them slip from your memory as long as you live, but teach them to your children and to your children's children.

Deuteronomy 4:9

This learning experience aims to enable you:

TO KNOW	To uncover some of the biblical and theological foundations of catechetical ministry.
TO FEEL	To claim these biblical and theological foundations for catechetical ministry as personally owned.
TO DO	To demonstrate the implications of catechetical ministry through the storytelling experience with elders.

Turn to the "Personal Responses" on pages 79-80.

INITIATION: Interviewing an Elder

Prior to gathering for the study of this new chapter, participants are invited to go and interview an elder of the community. Grandparents, retired persons, seniors chatting on park benches, family members, or neighbors could be informally approached and invited, with care, to share their responses to a simple interview.

In your interview, feel free to select one (or more) of the following questions to guide your conversation together, or compose your own questions. Be attentive to the words, gestures, folk expressions, and feelings of the elder. A cassette recorder would be helpful in capturing the spontaneity of the interviewing moment. However, make every effort in your manner to see to it that the senior is comfortable and not unduly pressured.

Suggested interview questions:
- If your life-journey were divided into five major chapters of your book of life, what would the titles of each chapter be?
- How would you like to be remembered?
- Compose an epitaph for your tombstone in your own personal style.

The opening of this learning session could very well be a sharing of the various interview experiences and the actual responses of the elders themselves.

PRESENTATION: The *Griot*

In Afrikan communities, the elders and the *griot* (pronounced GREE-oh) were the custodians of the collective story, the history, the customs, and the values of their people. Alex Haley, author of *Roots,* was able to recover his historic rootage through the memory of a *griot* who had received from the previous generations the story of Kunta Kinte. Together we will explore the rich implications of this storyteller tradition for today's proclamation of the Word.

If you participate in the life of a parish or are a member of a religious community, prayer group, or small Christian fellowship, perhaps you could plan an "Elder Day." (Suggestions are made in the CELEBRATION section of this chapter.)

For this occasion, you could invite some of the elder members of your congregation or community to share with the "children" (all those younger in age than they) some of their wisdom, "mother-wit," folktales, jokes, visions about life, stories about their pilgrim journey, and art, crafts, games, or photographs. This author once learned more than a dozen ways to creatively use a corncob!

The truth is that if our elders did not exist, we would not exist. Each of us draws from the old among us, not only our history, but the energy we need to live into the future. We draw from them the strength, insight, boldness, and the light needed to pass on to our children and to their children—an empowering heritage.

The wisdom spoken of here is not solely intellectual wisdom, but rather, insight into life itself. We have called this unique wisdom "mother-wit"—that familiar capacity to understand when other people are cornered by life's circumstances, to guide the young through life's ups and downs, to travel with suffering, to see God moving and acting in life's troubles, to experience joy in the morning.

Unfortunately, cherishing elders is contrary to America's cultural norms. We tend to relegate seniors to nursing homes, prompted by a cultural mentality which exalts youthfulness. We tend to mentally "exterminate" them because, reputedly, they are useless and a burden to society: they do not produce. Our society is heavy, indeed, with the sin of ageism.

Gospel-centered people have to lift up a new way of looking at the old. We have to take them seriously. Reverence them. For indeed, they are the custodians of our culture as well as custodians of our religious traditions.

Catechist as Storyteller

> Wherever we discover a living and active faith in Jesus Christ, we will also discover a community endeavoring to keep that faith alive (and pass it on).
> John H. Westerhoff III
> *Will Our Children Have Faith?*

As persons called and commissioned as teaching ministers within the Church, we are properly called *catechists.* Meanings are suggested by this word that are not completely satisfied by the word *teacher.* The fact is that the catechist exercises a ministry within the Church's life much richer and more penetrating than that of simply a teacher. The catechist certainly draws upon many of the concepts that shape what a teacher is and does, however. In order to arrive at a fuller appreciation of the distinctiveness of the word and ministry of the *catechist,* let us take a look at the term's origins and meanings.

The word *catechist* is rooted in the word *catechesis* which is an ancient word that frequently appears in the documents of the Church. It is derived from a Greek verb, *katéchein,* which means "to resound," "to echo," or "to hand down." These word roots imply oral instruction. The New Testament refers to instruction given to persons much like milk (rather than solid food) is given to small children (Heb. 5:12-14; 1 Cor. 3:1-3).

An echo is not a new word; it is the original word heard in different times and places. A catechist is the one who "resounds" or "resonates" the Word of God in the Scriptures and in the Word-made-flesh.

The Second Vatican Council places catechesis within the "ministry of the Word." Contemporary religious educators such as Berard Marthaler and John H. Westerhoff III are striving to expand the meaning of catechesis beyond oral instruction or handing down, to include a process whereby individuals are initiated and socialized in the church community. In other words, *catechesis* is a rich word which could aptly describe the process of *Christian becoming.*

Catechists, as teaching ministers, are very much like the *griots*. Catechists minister to the tribe-community in much the same way as our elders and ancestors have faithfully ministered to us. Catechists could easily be referred to as one of the key custodians of the consciousness, values, beliefs, way of life, rituals, and traditions of the Christian community.

The Black poet Claude McKay once wrote: "Gather the children together and tell them the story of their Blood!"

The catechist, as minister of the Word, could well be viewed as one of the principal storytellers of the believing community. The catechist him/herself has personally encountered the Story; he/she has personally experienced the storytelling community and is commissioned by that same community to sustain that Story in the community's memory and to pass it on to coming generations.

The catechist or pastoral minister has personally encountered the Story. This living Story is not something you organize and plan to tell and re-tell, but it is something you feel, something which gives life, which motivates and urges you onward. Furthermore, the Story gives you just what you need in order to deal with life's struggles, hardships, and questions. This Story is *your* Story. It is not just a story that has been passed on by tradition, parents, a priest, or a sister. It is a Story you have gratefully claimed as your own. It is an old Story interpreted for a new day.

Questions for Personal and Group Reflection

How can I discover the storyteller in me? Do I go to a workshop? Can I find a book or film on the subject? What curriculum is available on the telling of stories?

The key to an effective teaching ministry is the capacity to recall *your own* story. Take a moment to reflect on these questions: *What people have touched my life? How did I grow up? What are the significant moments in my adult life? How have these moments affected my faith in the Lord? Recalling the emphasis of Black Christian education on Scripture, what memories do I have of the Bible? What biblical images or stories best describe my life? Do I go to the Bible and embrace my faith in the midst of hardship and trouble?* Note some of the significant memories of your story.

Where can I go to nurture the storytelling gift? Besides my own experience, I must listen to the stories and insights of others. Take a look around your community. Look at the elders as well as the silent and unsung persons in the pews of our churches. Each one of them carries memories. *Are there persons in your church or learning community who stand as living reminders of Jesus Christ? Are there persons who warmly radiate when they speak about their faith?* List the names of those special people who come to your mind.

INTEGRATION: Honoring the Elders

We who today participate in the history and present reality of the Black church must be ever grateful to our ancestors' living witness to God's creation, providence, and power to save. Without a doubt, Black folk would have ceased to exist as a people if the Black church had not been our continual spiritual home.

Make plans to organize and celebrate an "Elder Day." (See pages 77-78 for suggestions.) After the celebration of Elder Day, come together as catechists and prayerfully reflect on your life-experiences with elders.

- *What memories do you carry of your experiences with elders?*
- *What role do you see elders playing in the expression of Black church?*
- *In what ways have elders ministered to you in your life?*
- *How have you ministered to elders?*
- *Identify concrete ways to deepen and further your outreach to the elders in your community.*

Some of these persons may have long been members of fraternal organizations, such as the Knights and Ladies of St. Peter Claver. You might never think of some who are members of your church organizations as "custodians of culture," but they provide a link to the past and a connection to our future. Talk to some of these persons formally and informally. Get to

know them as persons of faith. Don't dismiss them simply because they do not articulate what we have come to know as a contemporary model of the Church. Instead, strive to discover what stories, biblical images, and faith experiences touch and enliven them.

Catechist as Minister

The National Catechetical Directory, a basic Catholic document, focuses attention on the catechist's ministry as best understood in the context of Jesus' mission.

> Like other pastoral activities, catechetical ministry must be understood in relation to Jesus' threefold mission. It is a form of the *ministry of the word,* which proclaims and teaches. It leads to and flows from the *ministry of worship*, which sanctifies through prayer and sacrament. It supports the *ministry of service,* which is linked to efforts to achieve social justice and has traditionally been expressed in spiritual and corporal works of mercy (#32).

The goal of the catechist's ministry in the Church is to awaken and develop an active faith in Jesus. In other words, our aim is to enable adult believers to claim their faith as owned, that is, truly theirs. Essentially we aim toward calling the folk to the converted life.

Catechists are ministers in their own right. In many urban communities where the absence of ordained ministers and religious seems to be frequent, we must be careful not to suggest that lay persons who serve the local or diocesan church as catechists are merely temporary substitutes for priests and sisters. Quite the contrary is true. Baptism extends to every Christian the responsibility, right, and great privilege to share faith according to one's charism. Therefore, we can conclude that the ordinary ministers are the baptized; the "extraordinary" ministers are the ordained priests.

As Catechists the Church Calls You to Be . . .

Persons of Faith
How is my faith life? Am I willing to enable my learners to grow and mature as persons of faith involved in the constant process of growing in faith? No amount of competency training or technical expertise can make up for a lack of living faith in the catechist.

Witnesses of the Gospel
Catechists minister in the name of the Church and as witnesses of the Christian message. Do I believe in Gospel Power which is able to change the lives of real folk (especially mine!)? Am I able to see connections between my daily life and the message of Jesus Christ?

Witnesses of the Church
Catechists do not serve in isolation, but share in the total educational mission of the Church. Catechists must believe in the Church (the visible community of Jesus) and its constant need for renewal and conversion.

Proclaimers of the Message
Catechists must have a personal relationship with Jesus rooted in prayer. Catechists must strive to become more acquainted with the Bible through study, prayer, reflection. Catechists must be informed of the way in which the Church is growing in its understanding of God's revelation for each generation.

Sharers in the Fellowship of the Spirit
Catechists must be involved visibly in the ongoing life of the parish family. Catechists must develop among themselves a family and cooperative spirit.

Servants of the Community
"I have come not to be served, but to serve," teaches Jesus. If we do our ministry well, we are truly servants of the people. As a catechist, I will not only respond to needs when asked, but take the initiative to search out individual and community needs.

CELEBRATION: Celebrating with Elders

It is traditional that elders are honored and revered within the Black church. As mothers and fathers of the church, deacons, missionaries, teachers, leaders of prayer, and church organization captains, these senior members of the church family are recognized as essential pillars of the community. Unable to achieve status in many arenas and institutions of American life, Black elders have been frequently the prime forces behind the survival of the Black church.

Plan to celebrate the lives of the elders of your community. Make plans toward the honoring of those who have lived and served faithfully over the long haul.

Identify several senior persons who serve as mentors, role models, and nurturers for each participant in this learning experience.

Select a date convenient especially for the aged. Certain days of the week and times are prohibitive for some of the elderly due to the inconvenience of public transportation or the lack of safety on the streets.

Send a letter or invitation to the elders to be honored requesting their presence.

Conceivably, some of the bases that must be touched will be:
- order of ceremonies
- environment and space arrangement
- transportation needs for elders or their friends and families
- refreshments
- guest list and hospitality
- special needs (e.g., provisions for the disabled for easy accessibility to the celebration space, etc.)

The celebration of elders could include a time for storytelling such as "I was there" testimonies. The public library will gladly cooperate with your group in the acquisition of a historically significant front page of an old newspaper which can be enlarged to make a beautiful mural backdrop for the setting. During the celebration itself, the elders can freely share on-the-spot memories of the newspaper headlines.

Since many elders can fruits and vegetables, enjoy sports, or have interesting hobbies and crafts, an exposition of some of the expressions of their lives might additionally be planned as part of the celebration. The elders themselves might explain to the gathered assembly their personal involvement and interest in the activities.

Such a local celebration could well become a new "tradition." By celebrating the role of the old within our midst, we will begin to change some of the discriminatory attitudes toward them.

At the conclusion of the Elder Day, conduct a simple worship service in which the elders themselves can take an active role as leaders of prayer and song.

Environment: Prepare a cheerful environment using bright, fresh flowers and plants. Arrange the seating so that the elders can see, hear, and move easily.

Order of Service:

Keep the worship service simple and unburdened with structure.

Select a reading from the Scriptures which is one of the elders favorites, or you may read Psalm 71.

Make use of a *contemporary reading* such as the following quote from an Afrikan elder named Naana:

> (Let us never forget that) fruit is not the gathered
> gift of the instant but seed hidden in the earth, and
> tended and waited for and allowed to grow.
> Ayi Kwei Armah,
> *Fragments*

Present each elder with a bouquet of flowers, a corsage, or a boutonniere during the worship service.

RESPONSE: The Story Retold

Like the Afrikan *griot,* catechists are ministers of the community's story. By way of their distinctive calling within the Church's life, they are engaged in the service of enabling Christians to become more fully human, rooted persons and persons of faith.

Commissioned by the local church community, the catechist-servant must be a person of faith in order to effectively witness to the Gospel and to lift up a reviving word for a weary people. Called forth by the community, the catechist, like Jesus, invites his/her people to see their dying and rising in relationship to the dying and rising of Jesus.

Therefore, the catechist must be thoroughly and professionally prepared for this ministry but must speak to the hearts of the people like a poet, an elder, someone who loves them dearly.

Personal Responses

1) To nurture my storytelling skills I have decided to . . .

2) My involvement in Christian education increasingly is becoming an authentic ministry for me because . . .

3) My greatest difficulty or frustration as a minister of the Word is . . .

4) The age groups I tend to work with most effectively are . . .

TEACHING / LEARNING RESOURCES

BOOKS
Armah, Ayi Kewi. *Fragments.* New York: Collier Books, 1971.

Dunning, James B. *Ministries: Sharing God's Gifts.* Winona, MN: Saint Mary's Press, 1980.

Hater, Robert J. *The Ministry Explosion.* Dubuque: William C. Brown Co., 1979.

Kornhaber, A. and Woodward, K. *Grandparents/Grandchildren: The Vital Connection.* New York: Anchor Press/Doubleday, 1981.

Mitchell, Henry H. *The Recovery of Preaching.* New York: Harper & Row, 1977.

Mongoven, Anne Marie, OP. *Signs of Catechesis.* New York: Paulist Press, 1979.

Nouwen, Henri. *Aging.* Garden City, NY: Doubleday, 1976.

_____ . *Creative Ministry.* Garden City, NY: Doubleday, 1971.

Westerhoff III, John H. *Will Our Children Have Faith?* New York: Seabury Press, 1976.

ARTICLES
Jones, Nathan. "Evangelization in the Black Community." *City of God: Journal of Urban Ministry,* Winter 1980.

Haggerty, Brian A. "Martin Luther King, Jr.: Role Model for Religious Educators." *Religious Education,* January/February 1978.

Hater, Robert J. "Catechetical Ministry." *Catechist,* April 1979.

"Message to the Black Church and Community." Black Theology Project, Room 349, 475 Riverside Drive, New York City, NY 10027.

Westerhoff III, John H. "A Necessary Paradox: Catechesis and Evangelism, Nurture and Conversion." *Religious Education,* July/August 1978.

PERIODICALS
Storyfest Quarterly. Published by: Dr. Robert Bela Wilhelm, 4912 California Street, San Francisco, CA 94118. Subscription: $4.00 annually.

MEDIA

"Evangelization: Reflections on Living the Word." A filmstrip with accompanying record or cassette. (TeleKETICS) Franciscan Communications Center, 1229 South Santee Street, Los Angeles, CA 90015.

Jones, Nathan. "Evangelization in the Black Community." National Catholic Reporter Cassettes, P.O. Box 281, Kansas City, MO 64141.

Westerhoff III, John H. "The Pastoral Ministry of Education: Catechetics and Catechesis." National Catholic Reporter Cassettes, P.O. Box 281, Kansas City, MO 64141.

ORGANIZATIONS

National Association for the Preservation and Perpetuation of Storytelling (NAPPS), P.O. Box 112, Jonesboro, TN 37659.

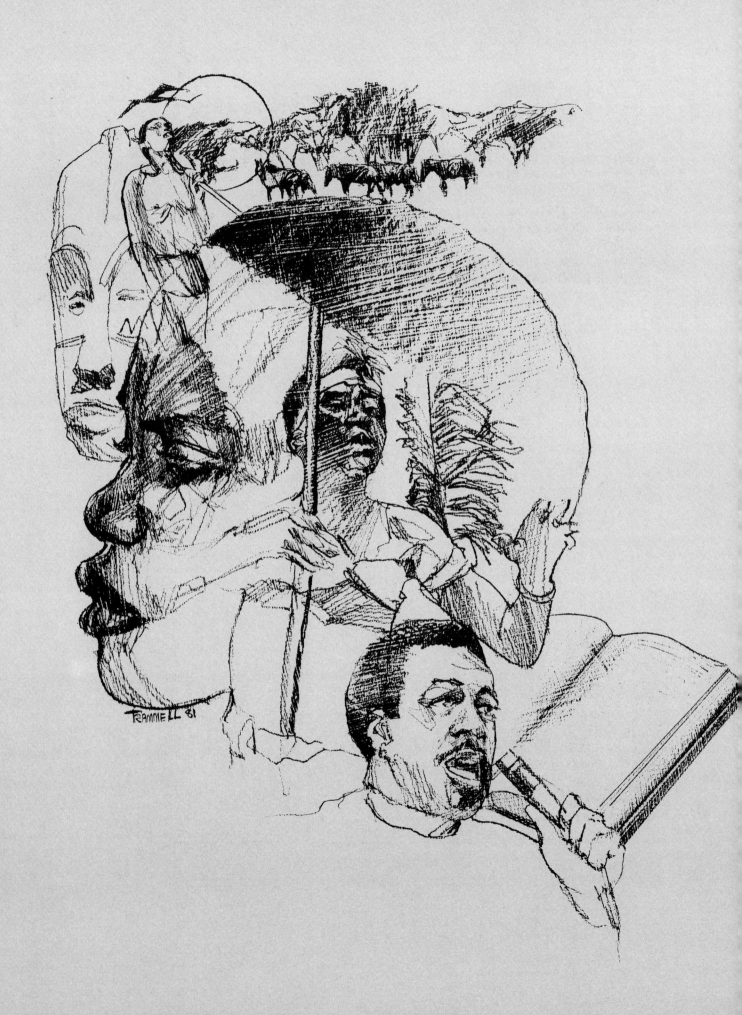

5
Sharing
the Old, Old Story

Each one of us has a story to tell. God is continually unfolding his revelation in our personal and collective lives. This process of reflection/action/reflection is aimed at identifying our story in God's Story and God's Story in ours.

For I want very much to see you,
in order to share a spiritual blessing
with you, to make you strong.
What I mean is that both you and I
will be helped at the same time,
you by my faith and I by your faith.

Romans 1:11-12

Simply stated, freedom is not doing what
I will but becoming what I should.

James H. Cone,
Black Theology and Black Power

This learning experience aims to enable you:

TO KNOW	To offer a fresh opportunity to explore ministry after the pattern of Jesus, through prayer, faith-sharing, and reflection.
TO FEEL	To deepen and intensify the learner's commitment to the Church's teaching ministry rooted in self-discovery.
TO DO	To enable the learner to acquire new skills in the communication of the faith and Black spirituality.

Turn to the "Personal Responses" on pages 90-91.

INITIATION: Claiming Your Story

An Exercise

Distribute a sheet of paper and a pen to each learner. Ask each participant to draw a series of three mountains on the paper in step-like fashion.

Focus on three key moments in your adult life: a sickness, a death, family struggles, a success, a life-crisis, a reunion, a birth, or a change of career or commitment.

Below are some questions which might be helpful to you as you proceed.

- How did that crisis, failure, joy, or memory challenge, reinforce, decrease, or strengthen your faith?

- How did that specific moment enable your faith to grow?

Spend a few minutes in silent reflection. Write down (or doodle) a word, phrase, or illustration that captures your faith-growth.

PRESENTATION: Testifying

Christians have been sharing testimonies, stories, and letters for a long time. Let us look at the biblical witness as exemplified in the writings of Paul the Apostle. Paul shares what Jesus Christ meant to him and to the growing churches. Paul shares his life, journeys, afflictions, and joys.

This is also true throughout the ages of Christian tradition. Augustine's *Confessions*, the legacy and writings of Teresa of Avila, and the diary of the desert hermit Charles de Foucauld, are testimonies. These were people who shared the testimony of what God was doing in and through their lives. The journal of the Quaker George Fox, the autobiography of the slave abolitionist Frederick Douglass—these too were the works of letter writers. Testifying may be somewhat new for us as contemporary Catholic-Christians, but on the other hand it is something that is very, very traditional. It is indeed old. And it is good.

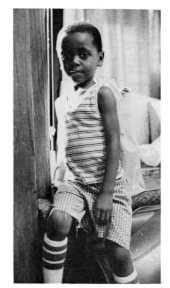

Do you recall stories that may have been told around your family dining table about relatives, family traditions, values, lost loves, dreams realized and deferred? Do you remember the jokes, folktales, ballads, prayers, rituals, or songs that were a vital part of your growing up?

Questions for Personal and Group Reflection

While gathered around your family feasting table, ask yourself: *How am I connected to the stories of my family and people? What feelings do these memories evoke?*

All of these experiences and memories can be life-giving, and the feelings they evoke can engender hope.

Culture

Our past as well as our present is always rooted in a culture. But what is "culture"?

When we speak of culture, we normally think primarily of art, music, food, drama, poetry, and dance. However, culture encompasses *everything* we do as a people:
- what we value;
- what we celebrate and how we celebrate;
- what we pass on as tradition;
- how we walk, talk, sing, and relate to one another;
- and, just as importantly, *how we look at God.*

Our cultural environment has shaped our

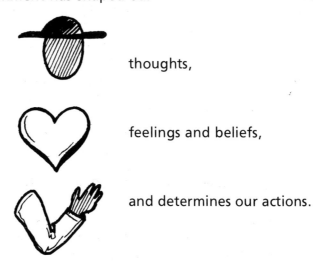

thoughts,

feelings and beliefs,

and determines our actions.

Culture includes such life-experiences as the way we have grown up, where we grew up, who raised us, what schools, churches, and community institutions we attended and participated in, what relationships we have cultivated, how we eat, what we eat, where we eat, and when we eat!

Culture embraces the total fabric of our lives. While this is certainly true, our Christian perspective does not view culture as an absolute, without "spot or wrinkle" or beyond critique. Yet through it all, each of us can only humanly look at God through human eyes.

To say it yet another way, "everything Black ain't good; everything Brown ain't good; everything White ain't good." All our cultural ways must stand under the judgment and challenge of the Gospel, the Church's tradition, and the ongoing revelation of God in his people. The way we look at God is determined most basically by *who* we are.

The National Catechetical Directory for Catholics affirms: "Today, the United States appears to be growing in appreciation of cultural diversity, recognizing the splendid beauty of all races, cultures, and ethnic groups" (#13).

Everyone Has a Story to Tell

Many of us look at our past history with a great deal of pride. The memories are wonderful, the experiences enriching, the hardships accepted, the mistakes healed. We have essentially embraced the beauty and the goodness, the chaos and the pain.

In our urban communities we are accustomed to seeing folk hanging out on the streetcorners. If you were to go up to some brother on the streetcorner who was into shooting dope or who carried a bottle in his hip pocket and ask, "What is God doing in your life?" he would laugh and say, "You must be crazy!"

Denial and rejection of one's life-story touches not only persons alienated from our churches but also members of our local congregations. Many of us, too, are not at home with our past. There are many wounds, psychological scars, harsh and unfriendly memories that we would prefer to forget. Sometimes the pain is too much to uncover again. Lifting up my burdens to God is healing. To speak my pains and fears in a trusting community is healing. **When I freely share my weaknesses with others I know and trust, these weaknesses can be transformed into strengths and power for new life.**

Testifying has been a tradition of the Black church in the United States, and as religious educators we can gain much by discovering the richness of this communal storytelling experience.

I can remember as a child being taken by my mother to testifying services at the local church. In the midst of a singing, shouting, hand-waving, and rejoicing community, persons moved by the Spirit would stand and say, "Giving honor and glory to God, my beloved pastor and his associates, members, and guests. Tonight I'm just mighty privileged to be able to stand here and tell the world that it pays to serve Jesus. I just want to tell everybody that my God is a way-maker . . . He's a way out of no-way."

In support of this testimony, members of the assembly would call out profound "amen's" or "tell the story!" Some would be moved to tears by a sister's or brother's story. But within this loving, nurturing fellowship, folk knew it was all right to break down and cry, to stomp one's feet, to wave one's hand, or even to jump for joy. It was all right. Everyone seemed to understand.

During these memorable moments of testifying, an oppressed people were able to release burdens, fears, pains (passing and historic), questions, and unending joy. For Black folk, these experiences within the life of the church-family were an emotional and spiritual purgative.

Five days a week, Joe Jones has been considered a nobody in his working situation—illiterate, overweight, rejected. But on Sunday morning, Joe Jones puts on his suit and tie, steps into his church and is known as "Deacon Jones." He has become *somebody*. In the midst of a loving community, Deacon Jones is a person. Therefore, he just has to shout! He just has to clap his hands, moan, and cry! Waving his hands and dancing for joy, he gives full expression to the old, old Story.

The gathered community would say, "Amen, Deacon Jones. Amen! Keep on telling the Story. Let him use you. We know what ya talkin' 'bout . . . just let go and let God!"

IN LETTING GO, Black people were able to cast off:

SLAVE NAMES	"niggah"	"bitch"
SLAVE IDENTITY	"uncle"	"gal"
THE OLD SELF	"boy"	"auntie"
THE OLD WINESKIN	"baby"	

IN LETTING GOD, Black people assumed:

A NEW NAME	*the*
A NEW IDENTITY	*people*
A NEW FEELING ABOUT THEMSELVES	*of*
A NEW BEAUTY	*God*

No longer was Joe Jones a "boy" in a racist world, but rather someone claimed and named by a saving God. He had a new name, a new walk, a new talk.

I recall sharing the story of Deacon Jones in a religious education workshop. A White catechist jumped up saying, "Oh, Black people have such cute sayings and poetry!"

I found myself laughing and retorted, "Don't be fooled by 'cute poetry.' What you're hearing in these stories is a deep and living theology." The catechist looked quite puzzled as if to say, "Well, I never thought Black people were theological."

That was the opening I needed to guide this person to better understand that the "cute poetry" was really the testimony of a people made new in Christ Jesus. In a lively way, these stories testify to what our church is called to witness. In fact, the aim of everything we do in our churches—our worship, community, learning, service—is toward the converted life of the person and the entire Body. If we are born again in Christ Jesus, we are indeed a new creation.

INTEGRATION: A New Name

I remember a woman who once told me upon leaving a Catholic church in New York, "Nathan, every time I leave this church I feel clean all over!" In that church she had experienced an emotional and spiritual cleansing. A renewal. A revival. A realization came over her that "I can" when everybody else says, "I can't."

Black elders, like this New York woman, have traditionally celebrated the **conversion-experience** in storytelling, nurturing fellowship, and song. Their words echo through generations of dark valleys. These songs, like the one here, give testimony to the hope that is ever within us.

Tell me how did you feel
When you come out of da wilderness?
Did your soul get happy?
Did you love everybody?

I looked at my hands;
My hands looked new.
I looked at my feet;
And they did, too!

Does this song echo in your own life?

The aim of catechesis is the converted life (a changed heart and mind) of the person and the Church.

Questions for Personal and Group Reflection

What aspects of my own life are yet in need of conversion? How's my faith life? Where in my life do I need to let go and let God? Where am I standing in the need of prayer?

Christian discipleship means a new name, a new vision, a new attitude, a new walk, and a new talk. *Is this song merely poetry, or do these words resonate within you?* Share your testimony with someone.

CELEBRATION: Inspiring Faith

All participants should move into a new, prayerful environment which has been prepared beforehand.

As a candle burns, the opened Bible is turned to Paul's first letter to the Thessalonians:

> So well disposed were we to you, in fact, that we wanted to share with you not only God's tidings but *our very lives,* so dear had you become to us (2:8).

After a few moments of silence, someone moved by God's Spirit will lead the community in a prayer of thanksgiving for the testimonies of our lives. In response, someone might want to lead a congregational hymn. Or a recording of the spiritual "I Told Jesus Be Alright If He Changed My Name" could be played or another appropriate hymn.

The worship service concludes with a prayer of blessing led by a prayer leader in the group.

RESPONSE: Cherishing the Faith

Each of us carries within us the old, old Story. Our abundant God is unfolding his revelation to us and to our community at every moment. Throughout this learning experience of reflection/action/reflection, we have, hopefully, discovered a fresh perspective on this old, old Story. Now, for us, this Story can be claimed as ever new.

Through a process of life reflection and introspection, we have sought to uncover God's movement in our personal histories as well as in our present hour. Christians recognize that revelation is not static but dynamic, ongoing. God is revealing himself even as we gather together for this learning experience. Not only are we called to share this Word with others, we must identify, claim, and cherish the Word within *us.* We do not want to preach a gift that we have not begun to claim and fully accept for ourselves.

If our churches and communities of faith are to be unfailing places of healing, living water, nourishment, and nurturance, we must necessarily move one another nearer and nearer **toward a personal encounter with the Lord.**

If we are to be faithful to the Gospel mandate, we must also endlessly struggle **to build up and participate in the body of Christ, the Church,** wherever we are. Christian communities can provide the healing dimension for all of life's pains.

Finally, in order to be credible to this age and to bring about God's Kingdom, we must move **toward transforming society.**

To be an authentic witness of God's saving Word among Black folk of faith, each of these focal dimensions must embrace us and we must embrace them.

Personal Responses

1) One moment in which I recently experienced the presence of the living God in my own life was . . .

2) I look upon my racial, ethnic, and cultural background with feelings of . . .

3) I feel "brand new" in my church when . . .

4) The most satisfying experience for me in a Black worshiping community was . . .

TEACHING / LEARNING RESOURCES

BOOKS

Amini, Johari. *An African Frame of Reference.* Chicago: Third World Press, [1972?].

Cone, James H. *God of the Oppressed.* New York: Seabury Press, 1975.

Keen, Sam. *Telling Your Story.* New York: Signet Books, 1973.

Lester, Julius. *To Be a Slave.* New York: Dial Press, 1968.

Sawyer, Ruth. *The Way of the Storyteller.* New York: Penguin Books, 1970.

Shea, John. *Stories of Faith.* Chicago: The Thomas More Publishers, 1980.

Wilmore, Gayraud. *Black Religion and Black Radicalism.* New York: Anchor/Doubleday, 1973.

ARTICLES

Cone, James H. "Santification, Liberation and Black Worship." *Theology Today,* [date unavailable].

Jones, Nathan. "The Church: A Storytelling Community." *The Catechist,* April 1979.

Parabola Magazine. Special Issue on Storytelling and Education. November 1979. Available from: 150 Fifth Avenue, New York City, NY 10011.

Shea, John. "And the Jesus Said . . . Christian Storytelling and Personal Spirituality." *New Catholic World,* March/April 1979.

MEDIA

"The Dancing Prophet." 16mm film with guide. (TeleKETICS) Franciscan Communications Center, 1229 South Santee Street, Los Angeles, CA 90015.

Flack, Roberta. "First Take." Album. (See especially the cut entitled "I Told Jesus.") New York: Atlantic Recording Corp., 1969.

"To Tell of Gideon: The Art of Storytelling in the Church." Book with record or cassette. Published by: John and Mary Harrell, Box 9006, Berkeley, CA 94709.

6
Program Planning for the Black Church

Planning helps to prevent failure. Program planning is an essential under-pinning of any effective catechetical ministry. The vision or affirmation which animates this programming is of equal importance. We must articulate, review, and critique our assumptions and plans.

And the Lord answered me:
"Write the vision;
make it plain upon tablets,
so he may run who reads it.
For still the vision awaits its time;
it hastens to the end—it will not lie.
If it seems slow, wait for it;
it will surely come, it will not delay."

Habakkuk 2:2-3

Christianity is not taught so much as caught.
That was certainly true in the first century.
Men had the Christian faith transmitted to
them through their experience with the community
of faith. The distinguishing mark of the early
Church was not its verbal message (words),
its preaching and teaching, but its non-verbal
message (the Word), and its style of life.

John H. Westerhoff III
Values for Tomorrow's Children

This learning experience aims to enable you:

TO KNOW
To acquire and sharpen some basic skills in catechetical programming and design for adults, youth, and children.

TO FEEL	To take an inner look at one's capacity to be deeply in touch with the lives and stories of the learning community.
TO DO	To design, critique, and evaluate an effective catechetical ministry for your local community.

Turn to the "Personal Responses" on page 102.

INITIATION: Two Teams of Warriors

There is an Afrikan story that tells of two teams of warriors who were sent away from their village in search of a new clearing where the soil was more fertile and the harvests would be more fruitful. After making it successfully through a particularly difficult portion of the journey, the first team of warriors buoyed themselves up with optimism. They had already gone through the thickest of forests, they reasoned, and so they trudged ahead, neither looking behind them to see how they had made it thus far nor making special preparations for what they might find ahead. They had goals, but they had no special plans—or tactics—for reaching their goals. For them, the remainder of the journey was long, difficult, and endless.

The second team of warriors was wiser than the first in several major ways. With each step forward, they looked back to study the techniques they had used to wade through dangerous waters and slash through undergrowth. When they celebrated their successes, they gave thanks to the Good Spirit for their solidarity and unity. When they passed through a most difficult part of the journey, they did not predict what lay ahead for them. They were optimistic only about their ability to handle future problems *together* because they had studied the keys to their past success together. For them, the major question was not, "What shall we find ahead?" but rather, "How do we prepare ourselves now for whatever lies ahead?" They prepared for those who would follow.

Below are some questions which can help you reflect on this story of the two teams of warriors.

1) Which team of warriors do I most immediately identify with and why?

2) My teaching ministry most reflects the attitudes and behavior of which team of warriors? Am I comfortable with this?

3) An honest reading of the condition of Black people today and the mission of the Church relays certain messages to me as a catechist. Identify these messages.

PRESENTATION

A Checklist for Planning

☐ BEGIN WITH YOUR VISIONS
- What is it that we want the adults, youth, and children of our church . . .
    - TO KNOW?
    - TO FEEL?
    - TO DO?

☐ STUDY YOUR CONGREGATION
- Develop a membership file:
    - How many adults, youth, children are we addressing?
    - What are these persons like?
    - What is our larger community like?
    - What is going on educationally in our parish?
    - What are the strengths/weaknesses of our educational ministries?
    - Where are the gaps in these programs?
    - How are these programs organized?
    - What financial resources are available?
    - What leadership resources are available?

☐ WHAT DO WE WISH TO DO?
- Initiate a process of study in order to explore the meaning of catechesis in the context of the needs of our local church.
- Set goals (*what* we wish to accomplish).
- Set objectives (*how* we wish to accomplish our goals).

☐ EXPLORE EDUCATIONAL POSSIBILITIES
- Study various ways of doing Christian education:
    Wholistic: The total life, worshiping, preaching, witnessing, and service of the congregation *is* Christian education. Education and formation in faith is the responsibility of the total parish community.

Catechesis builds on the life-experiences of the people in their homes, in the streets, on their jobs, in their neighborhoods.

Intergenerational: Educational programming is organized across age lines. The entire parish community learns together in family clusters or learning teams. We live together—not in separate communities divided by generations, but rather in merged communities spanning generations. This inter-age grouping should be reflected in our educational design.

Graded: Traditionally we have divided ages and groups based on the schooling model. However, there are certain times when a certain catechesis is more appropriate to one age group than to another. The graded approach provides for this.

Learning centers: A variety of creative learning activities are available to enable learners to accomplish the given aims of the catechesis in ways which are individually suitable.

Liberation-oriented education: Learners are engaged in the transformation of their parish life by a process of critical reflection/action rooted in biblical faith and informed through catechesis. Persons are viewed as conscious beings and not objects. Persons are responsible for their personal growth in faith and the collective growth of the parish. Catechesis is aimed toward a converted life and a commitment to free the oppressed wherever they might be. Catechists enter into dialogue with the learners and view their role as ministers, enablers, resources.

☐ EXPLORE TIMES AND SETTINGS
- Sundays:
   Sunday School
   lectionary-based Bible study
   liturgical season formation
   afternoon learning experience
- During the Week:
   midweek Bible study
   released-time classes
   storytelling experience
   after-school religious education followed by dinner
   retreats at home; retreats at church
   action-oriented learning; learning by doing
- Vacation:
   Bible school (for all ages) which meets in the evening and includes light supper, prayer, message, celebration.
   Church retreats in the country with opportunities for "down home" camp meetings, fellowship meals, Bible study, liturgy.
- Bible and Culture School:
   Catechesis and its relationship to Black heritage and culture is affirmed (e.g., one hour of Bible, doctrine, liturgy; one hour of related Black cultural experiences). The integral relationship of faith and the culture of the people is the aim.

- Retreats:

  Get-away days or weekends to pray can be excellent learning opportunities for all ages. Structured times for prayer, meals, and creative learning can enable this time to be different from other learning situations in the church.

  Such retreats (or workshops) could be held in homes, senior citizen centers, church, or retreat houses.
- Congregational Meetings:

  The entire parish community is invited to an information-sharing fellowship. News. Criticism. How we can collectively grow.

☐ HOW DO WE BUILD OUR CURRICULUM?

- **Using and adapting existing materials:** How can these tools enable us to achieve our catechetical goals more effectively? What changes will have to be made?
- **Discovering new materials:** Your local diocesan office of religious education provides services in the professional selection of teaching/learning materials.
- **Developing our own curriculum:** Organize around themes related to real life (such as crime and violence in the city, family life, economic power, identity), biblical story (how God *has* acted and *is* acting among his people), and Catholic-Christian tradition (unique ways we have of living, expressing, and witnessing that Jesus is Lord).

☐ SELECTING RESOURCES

- People are the most vital resources.
- Role and function of resources.
- Varieties of resources available to the church:

  people (speak with the elders, persons in pews with different talents, diocesan office personnel).

  institutional (other local churches, schools, area colleges, community centers, community organizations, and national organizations).

  materials (Bibles, books, periodicals, films, filmstrips, poetry, music, puppets, movies, TV, learning games).

☐ ONGOING CATECHIST FORMATION

- Identification of gifted persons, trained as catechists, ministers of the Word.
- Support is offered these catechists through ongoing training sessions in local parishes, in parish clusters, or on the diocesan level.
- Times and occasions to celebrate the services of these catechists should be planned.
- Development of support services: home visitors, audio-visual specialists.

☐ EVALUATION

- Did we accomplish the goals originally set forth?
- Specify the ways and experiences through which these goals were accomplished.

- What are adults, youth, and children of our parish now thinking? feeling? doing?
- What are the most positive features of our educational ministries? Why?
- What are the least admirable features of our programs? Why?
- What changes need to occur in our approach to Christian education; our models and programs; our teaching/learning techniques; our service efforts in the church and larger community; our training of catechists; our follow-up in the homes, school, community; our parish life; our liturgy; and our publicity and personal contact?

In the same manner as the second team of Afrikan warriors, we have taken a look at ourselves, our needs, and our resources through the prism of this checklist.

It is now the time to discover a new clearing where the harvest might indeed be more fruitful. By unearthing all of the above information and incorporating these insights into our teaching/learning designs, we will be prepared to move into our ministry better informed and more appropriately equipped and skilled.

In order to more seriously probe the individual and corporate significance of this chapter's presentation, it is suggested that the catechists be

divided according to either the age or grade level they teach or the interest area (e.g., primary grades, sacramental preparation, or adult formation.)

Each small interest group has the task of wrestling with the following questions (synthesized from "The Checklist for Planning") with attention given to the specific concerns of their constituency:

1) *What do we want the learners to know, feel, and do as a result of our total Christian education program design?*

2) *Describe in detail the learners themselves.*

3) *Describe in detail the gifts and weaknesses of the catechetical staff and related ministers or volunteers.*

4) *What specific educational approach have we decided to implement? Why?*

5) *What human resources as well as material resources are available to us?*

6) *Will we participate in ongoing training?*

7) *How shall we evaluate our teaching and programming in the light of our original vision?*

INTEGRATION: Our Own Affirmations

Take time now to focus on the vision behind all your planning. Read the thirteen "Affirmations of Black Christian Education" (which follow on p. 100) carefully and thoughtfully as a total learning community. Request that the catechists break up into small groups of three to five members. The task of the small groups will be to rewrite each of the affirmations using the language, idiom, symbols, and insights of their local community. The question for us to consider in this activity is: "How can these affirmations truly become *our own?*"

Following the discussion, a recorder comes forth from each group and shares the affirmations one by one. Someone should record these on newsprint so they are visible to all.

After each group has shared, the task remains to arrive at a consensus among all the catechists regarding each affirmation—its content and expression.

The assembly will make a circle (fishbowl) around the recorders, who are charged to discuss the affirmations until a consensus in language, style, and concept is reached. Remarks can be made by members of the larger body in order to move the consensus process along with questions, clarifica-

tions, and specifications. When a consensus is reached, these affirmations are then proudly proclaimed by the recorders.

The affirmations scroll is placed on a small table near the enthroned Bible and, if possible, each catechist approaches and signs his/her name on the sheet. Through this ritual action, all persons have the opportunity to publicly affirm these statements as objectives and visions which will inform their ministry in the Church. (See the culminating ritual suggested in the CELEBRATION section of this chapter.)

Affirmations of Black Christian Education

1) To affirm that all Black children, youth, and adults are human and can learn.
2) To affirm that all Black children, youth, and adults must be educated as members of a Black family, a Black community, and a community of faith.
3) To affirm that the education in faith of Black children, youth, and adults, wherever it takes place, should be controlled by Black people.
4) To design the educational experience around liberation-oriented goals and values.
5) To create an environment of love and an experience of belonging where children, youth, and adults can freely respond to God through Jesus Christ in faith and love.
6) To make connections between the agony and ecstacy of the Black experience and the Black struggle with the revelation of God in the Bible.
7) To uplift those values and principles of the Black experience that build a sense of familyhood among God's people.
8) To create opportunities in our learning situations for freedom and responsible action.
9) To equip children, youth, and adults to realize their God-given capabilities and to use them for the ultimate resurrection of our people.
10) To provide our children, youth, and adults with positive and life-giving images of Black manhood and womanhood.
11) To instill in Black children, youth, and adults faith to persevere, courage to resist oppression, and love that will lift them from oppression toward freedom.
12) To draw on the life-experiences of children, youth, and adults in the preparation of learning activities which will reflect the connection between daily living, worship, faith, community-building, and the living Word of God.
13) To always approach our learners—children, youth, and adults—ready and prepared to provide our very best as committed catechists. With the help of our never-failing God, we'll make it all right!

CELEBRATION: Ritualizing Our Vision

The celebration of this chapter's learning experience centers around the owning of the "Affirmations of Black Christian Education." During the INTEGRATION period of this session, persons were engaged in the rewriting of the affirmation statements in order to make these statements expressive of local realities.

A simple service of affirmation is planned which will include a ritual signing of the affirmations by each participating catechist.

The order of worship begins with a reverent lighting of a candle as the community stands in a circle with linked arms, singing. Scripture is solemnly proclaimed (1 Pet. 2:9-10) followed by a spontaneous invitation by the master catechist to come and sign the affirmation scroll as a public expression of your intention to implement this vision in your teaching.

The ritual concludes with the singing of a song of victory.

RESPONSE: Building Church Together

A focal concern in educational program planning for our churches is: How can we be Christians together?

In what ways can we so share faith, interpret the Word, teach the tradition, celebrate, and act together that Christian faith will be credibly embraced by the generations?

Will we dare imagine a new attitude and vision of the Church's educational ministry with a view toward calling the Black church to life?

Catechesis and catechetical program planning in the Black church must reflect the historic insight of the Black fathers and mothers who so shaped their faith communities that the faith was communicated in its integrity with a decided accent on Black life and survival in a strange and weary land.

When engaged in program planning in your local community, dream a little: What uncharted ways can we imagine which will enable *this* community of faith to grow toward the converted life? Dream and imagine boldly.

Dialogue regularly with the members of your congregation as well as other community persons vitally interested in the ongoing life and service of your church. Beyond your professionally discerned *prescriptive needs* of the congregation, spend time ascertaining the people's *felt needs.*

When your vision is shaped, your goals and objectives established, do not neglect to uncover the giftedness of your church membership in order to fulfill the many necessary ministries. Provide *training opportunities* for the many different catechetical ministers.

Lastly, do not fail to evaluate and review what is occurring (or not

occurring) in the life of your parish, especially regarding this distinctive view toward catechesis. Are persons knowing, interpreting, living, and doing God's Word, and are we collectively growing more deeply into God's love-life?

Personal Responses

1) I would describe our Christian education programs as . . .

2) To make our catechetical setting more conducive to growth in faith, we must . . .

3) My biggest frustration in ministry is . . .

4) My relationship with the other teachers is . . .

TEACHING / LEARNING RESOURCES

BOOKS

DeBoy, James J. *Getting Started in Adult Religious Education.* New York: Paulist Press, 1979.

Downs, Thomas. *The Parish as Learning Community.* New York: Paulist Press, 1978.

Goodwin, Bennie E. *Reflections on Education: Meditations on King, Freire, and Jesus.* Goodpatrick Publishers (45 North 21st Street, East Orange, NJ 07017), 1978.

Harris, Maria. *The DRE Book.* New York: Paulist Press, 1977.

Haughey, John C., ed. *The Faith That Does Justice.* New York: Paulist Press, 1977.

McBride, Alfred. *Creative Teaching in Christian Education.* Boston: Allyn and Bacon, 1978.

Perkins, Eugene. *Home Is a Dirty Street: The Social Oppression of Black Children.* Chicago: Third World Press, 1975.

Westerhoff III, John H. *Bringing Up Children in the Christian Faith.* Minneapolis: Winston Press, 1980.

_____ . *Inner Growth/Outer Change—An Educational Guide to Church Renewal.* New York: Seabury Press, 1979.

ARTICLES

Manternach, Janaan. "A No-Fail Recipe for Lesson Planning." *Religion Teacher's Journal,* November/December 1977, pp. 17-19.

_____ . "A Teacher's Guide to Creative Learning." *Religion Teacher's Journal,* September 1977, pp. 17-19.

MEDIA

Afro-Am Educational Materials for all ages. Afro-Am Publishing Co., 910 South Michigan Avenue, Suite 556, Chicago, IL 60605.

7
Catechesis for Liberation and Transformation

We cannot program faith-growth. However, we can facilitate religious awareness and formation through a learning process attuned to people's needs and the story of the faith. Designs for such a process are created in dialogue with the learning community, daily life, and the Church's tradition. This results in a truly creative, liberating, and transforming curriculum.

The people who walked in darkness
have seen a great light;
Upon those who dwelt in the land of gloom,
a light has shone.

Isaiah 9:1

Up, you mighty race!
You can accomplish what you will.

Marcus Garvey

This learning experience aims to enable you:

TO KNOW	To acquire some new skills and direction in the development of a catechetical curriculum for the Black community.
TO FEEL	To feel comfortable with the task of curriculum design through skill-building.
TO DO	To be capable of designing a curriculum model for the Black church based on the perspectives presented.

Turn to the "Personal Responses" on pages 112-113.

INITIATION: The World Community and Our Faith

An Exercise

Randomly select several key topics, issues, questions, problems, or concerns of your local community which are reflected in the people's talk, media, and other ways of communicating. Topics such as family violence in the city, family instability, inflation, unemployment, sickness, or the younger generation might be good starting points.

Flip through copies of the newspaper (including the local Black newspaper), magazines, and advertisements to locate pictures, words, phrases, stories, or symbols which capture or illustrate the topics you have selected. Perhaps you might wish to paste your illustrations on a poster board for use in a later group activity.

PRESENTATION: A Curriculum Model for Lesson Planning

Catechesis has the task of drawing persons ever more deeply into a fuller appreciation of the richness of the lifelong invitation to faith.

With a profound respect for unique cultural nuances, the source of catechesis is God's Word, fully revealed in Jesus Christ and at work in the lives of people exercising their faith under the guidance of the Church.

Further, the various manifestations of the source of catechesis are *signs* under four general headings: biblical signs, liturgical signs, ecclesial signs, and natural signs. Catechesis in the Black community must reflect these signs of God's self-revelation and also reflect lived, Black experience in the light of the signs. You will note themes in this chapter correlating to the foundational principles for Black Christian education (chapter 1).

Biblical Signs

Biblical signs consist of the varied and wonderful ways, recorded in Scripture, by which God reveals himself. Catechetical experiences should lead persons gradually, according to their readiness and capabilities, to a friendship with the biblical word and major themes in the whole Bible—the Hebrew Scriptures as well as the Christian Scriptures.

Liturgical Signs

The liturgy of the Church and its sacramental life are signs which mediate God's saving, loving power, making real the experiences they symbolize. The catechized community must increasingly grow in an awareness of the signs, symbols, actions, and expressions of the liturgy toward the goal of a fuller participation in the ecclesial community.

| **Ecclesial Signs** | Our teaching ministry recognizes the vital importance of creed, doctrine, and the testimony of Christian witness as integral to the total catechetical design. The Catholic *National Catechetical Di-* |

rectory points out that "the Church gives witness to its faith through its way of life, its manner of worship, and the service it renders" (#45).

Each lesson, whether with adults, youth, or children, should seek to more fully integrate the learners into a life-giving and life-saving church family through the example of both living and historic witnesses of faith. It is imperative that a significant number of these witnesses and ecclesial experiences reflect the specific race, culture, and environment of the catechized as well as introduce the learners to the multicultural face of the Church.

| **Natural Signs** | A close look at the people's lives—social, economic, and political condition—and the realities of the world community will provide fundamental approaches in our teaching. |

No human experience is alien to catechesis, for learners are prepared in the ecclesial community to examine all of life in the light of Christian faith.

A Teaching/Learning Model

What follows is a teaching/learning design generated out of pastoral sensitivity to the needs of many persons engaged in Christian-education ministries in the Black church who are searching for a helpful guide to curriculum and lesson planning.

The chart on the following page is created for use by catechists with adults, youth, or children. It is strongly suggested that each learning session include the specified steps in the "Growth-in-Faith Process." Each step is a vital movement from the initiation of the learning process in life-experience, to the sharing of tradition, to the biblical-liturgical proclamation, to the application to life (integration), and to the celebration. Every step along the process organically flows into the next and builds upon what has been previously uncovered.

The steps are:

> Life-Experience (natural signs);
> Tradition (biblical signs);
> Proclamation (liturgical signs);
> Integration (ecclesial signs); and
> Celebration.

As with every set of guidelines, it is necessary to adapt this "Growth-in-Faith Process" to your local needs, teaching objectives, and the pedagogical readiness of your learners.

Consistent with the Church's renewed appreciation of catechesis, well expressed in the *National Catechetical Directory,* these guidelines are reflective of the best of developmental psychology and pedagogy.

The second aspect of the "Growth-in-Faith Process" is the suggested "Strategies" for teaching/learning. Beneath each step in the catechetical process are techniques and hints toward the development of each particular step of the lesson. These strategies require both adequate preparation and a capacity for creativity on the part of the catechist.

It cannot be overly stressed how important prayer and study are in the preparation for the learning session. Looking ahead at forthcoming lessons and advance planning will provide the necessary span of time needed to search out tools and techniques to enrich the session. Advance planning will also enable the catechist to deepen his/her appreciation of the lesson's core message.

At the conclusion of each Christian education class, the teacher should spend some time in personal evaluation and assessment. Did learning happen? Did the learners enjoy the class? Did I enjoy the class? How could I have improved the session?

GROWTH-IN-FAITH PROCESS: A Teaching / Learning Process for Planning Sessions

LIFE-EXPERIENCE

1) Initiate the learning experience by taking an honest look at real, raw life.

2) Consider the issues, concerns, questions, and current events which touch upon the lives of the learners.

3) Evoke human experiences through physical activities, stories, music, interests, art, events, symbols, etc.

Suggested strategies (*Exploring*)
- stimulating inner exploration
- awakening interest
- recalling life-moments
- centering, focusing
- engaging in critical reflection
- creating a hospitable atmosphere

TRADITION

1) Learners are pointed toward truth by uncovering the sacred in life-experience, through the Bible, doctrine, Church tradition, Christian witness.

2) A focal insight of Christian faith is shared in order to learn something previously unknown or only dimly sensed.

3) The Word and tradition speak for themselves and seek a personal response.

Suggested strategies (*Sharing*)
- open sharing of a lived and living faith
- identifying "seeds of the Word" already present in daily life
- with sensitivity to developmental diversities among learners, a variety of teaching skills and aids can be employed enabling life-experience and tradition to be communicated effectively

PROCLAMATION

1) A liturgical proclamation of the message as recorded in Scripture.

2) We celebrate our unity around the Word.

3) The Word is proclaimed in a reverent manner.

Suggested strategies (*Announcing*)
- in a worshipful atmosphere, a candle is lit and the key biblical passage is proclaimed
- learners are gathered in a circle with joined hands

INTEGRATION

1) Linking the faith-tradition to human experience: "What could this mean to me?"

2) Identifying models of faith, especially Black heroes/**sheroes**.

3) A response-in-faith: uncovering ways to personally apply the message to life.

Suggested strategies (*Guiding*)
- an opportunity to verbalize their appreciation of the message
- a time for some creative expression of the message

CELEBRATION

1) Faith leads us to worship.

2) We celebrate our shared experience in prayer, worship, ritual, or other creative expression.

3) We give testimony to God's action in our lives *together*.

Suggested strategies (*Worshiping*)
- involve everyone in songs and expressive prayer, drawing together the learnings of each session into a joyous celebration

INTEGRATION: Connecting Faith to Life

Questions for Personal and Group Reflection

Move back to the posters you created at the opening of this session (see p. 106). Ask yourself: *In what concrete ways does my faith-confession provide an alternative, insight, direction, or clarity for me when faced with this kind of issue, problem, or crisis? How does Christian faith enable me to deal with crime, troubles, crises, or burdens? Does our faith and our catechesis equip us (and our learners) for life's battlefields? Does Christian faith offer an alternative to depression? Does Christian faith provide "a way out of no-way"? Does faith in Christ Jesus offer us a consciousness with which we can better cope with city noise, financial woes, or job insecurity?*

If our confession of Jesus does not have some word to utter in the midst of adult crises, family tensions, love hang-overs, and crime in the streets, then our faith is a sham or, biblically speaking, it is pharisaical.

An Exercise

Refer back to the diagram of a learning process (p. 109) which could easily be adapted to any age or grade level or interest group. Your task is to decide the specific age, grade, or context of the group. Isolate a theme from the life-experience of the class and begin working in small groups of four to five to develop a learning strategy for a class session. Encourage everyone to contribute their ideas freely to this joint project. (You might also want to refer to chapter 1 to refresh your memory of the foundational principles of Black Christian education.)

CELEBRATION: A Love Feast

Environment: Create a prayerful environment by burning incense and lighting a candle. When persons have settled, carry the Bible in procession proudly, placing it in a central position in the praying community. The love feast can proceed according to the following suggested order:

Order of Service:

Gathering hymn—"Blessed Assurance"
Call to worship—an invitation to pray with one's total being
Lighting of the festival candles—As each candle is reverently lit, the community prays the Black Christian Principles*:

---

*The Black Christian Principles are a creative appropriation of the Nguzo Saba (Seven Principles of Black Unity), originally formulated by Maulana Ron Karenga. These principles, though not an exhaustive listing, reflect life-values that are traditional among Afrikan peoples wherever they might be. Black Christians have attempted to perceive in these principles values that are consistent with Gospel and biblical values.

- Lord, we have risen this day in your light. We pray that all we are and all we do today will continue to draw us nearer and nearer to one another and to you—our way out of no-way.
- Teach us, Lord, to claim each day who we are and whose we are.
- Everything we do takes responsible work; everything else is jive.
- Our elders have taught us: "Each one, reach one."
- We all have a mission to change our condition.
- Create in us a new spirit, a new walk, a new talk.
- And, Lord, keep us on your battlefield, faithful to the end.

Opening prayer on bended knee—led by a community person
Response hymn—congregational hymn
Scripture reading—selected by the catechists
Silent reflection
Congregational response hymn
Testimonies—"What has this day meant for you?"
Intercessions—Is there a need in your life? in someone else's life?
Love feast—Baskets of cornbread and pitchers of lemonade are brought forth by appointed ministers. An elder comes to the center of the praying ground and lifts his/her hands and prays a blessing over the feast. Ministers bring food and drink to the tables. The sharing of the feast. A recording of meditative music is played during the love feast.
Silent meditation
Hymn of thanksgiving—"Blessed Assurance"

RESPONSE: The "Invisible" Leader

A leader is best
When people barely know that he exists,
Not so good when people obey and acclaim him,
Worst when they despise him.
'Fail to honor people,
They fail to honor you';
But of a good leader, who talks little
When his work is done, his aim fulfilled,
They will all say, 'We did this ourselves.'

These powerfully reflective lines are the poetry of the sixth century B.C. Chinese philosopher Lao Tzu. They communicate forcibly the goal to which all our catechetical skill-building is pointing: the ownership of the curriculum design and program by the people themselves.

As catechists, we are much like this model of leadership. We might be likened to "mystagogues" who gladly break open and unfold the great mysteries of faith to our people. The message we unfold, if received, enables a people to change their very lives.

Many of the learnings of the previous chapters have come to bear on this working session. You have experimented now with the praxis—the practical skills in curriculum design. What must be uppermost in our collective consciousness is that our task must be to enable people to invest time, energy, and conviction in the curriculum and, more importantly, in the eternal values to which the curriculum points.

Personal Responses

1) I find myself failing to plan in my ministry because . . .

2) Others have pointed out that my greatest strength as a catechist lies in . . .

3) The life-experience of my learners which critically demands reflection in the light of the Gospel is . . .

4) My learners are motivated for Christian education by . . .

5) My best quality as a leader is . . .

TEACHING / LEARNING RESOURCES

Books

Adebonojo, Mary. *Free to Choose: Youth Program Resources from the Black Perspective.* Valley Forge, PA: Judson Press, 1980.

Beissert, Marguerite R. *Intergenerational Manual for Christian Education, Shared Approaches.* New York: United Church Press, 1977.

Inter-religious Task Force for Social Analysis. *Must We Choose Sides?* (Study/Action Guide) The Task Force (464 19th Street, Oakland, CA 94612), 1979.

McCarthy, Estelle R. *Adults: A Manual for Christian Education/Shared Approaches.* Atlanta: General Assembly Mission Board, Presbyterian Church in the United States, 1977.

New Roads to Faith: Black Perspectives in Church Education (Monograph Series). Joint Educational Development, 1505 Race Street, Philadelphia, PA 19102. $1.65 per packet.

Russell, Joseph. *Sharing the Biblical Story.* Minneapolis: Winston Press, 1979.

ARTICLES

Black Books Bulletin. Special Issue on Black Religion. Spring 1976. Published by: Institute of Positive Education, 7524 South Cottage Grove Avenue, Chicago, IL 60619. $2.00 per copy.

Eugene, Toinette, PBVM. "City Lights: An Urban Spirituality." *City of God: A Journal of Urban Ministry,* Summer 1979.

MEDIA

Mongoven, Anne Marie, OP. "Signs of Catechesis: An Overview of the National Catechetical Directory." Filmstrip series kit. Paulist Press, 1979.